A GUIDE TO CAVES, MINES AND LAVA TUBES

California
UNDERGROUND
adventures

JON KRAMER AND JULIE MARTINEZ

Adventure Publications, Inc.
Cambridge, MN

author dedications

The most primal fear among cavers is the sudden and complete loss of light while deep underground. While I thankfully haven't been in such a situation, I've had close calls. At such times it is cathartic to have an emotional talisman which connects you to some form of lifeline. Mine takes the form of a beautiful jewel—my wife Julie—who renews and guides me by continually shining a hopeful light into the deepest abyss of my soul.

–Jon Kramer

To those first intrepid cavers who had the courage to descend into mysterious dark holes in the ground with nothing but simple lamps and candles and, as always, to my wonderful husband, Jon, who is continually teaching me new ways to enjoy the earth.

–Julie Martinez

special thanks

George Hecht and Hal Halvorson have been the most stalwart of friends both on rope and off. We also wish to thank Lisa Bolton and Sierra Nevada Recreation for her assistance and availability, John Fairchild, who led us on a world-class private tour of California Caverns, and many others, including: Stephen R. Fairchild at Boyden Cavern, Shaundy Francek at Black Chasm Cavern, Michael Miller at the Original 16:1 Mine, Elizabeth Stuart-Webb at the Eagle and High Peak Mine, Jim Allen at the Cave Store, Chris Boitano at Sutter Gold Mine, Randy Bolt at the California Mining and Mineral Museum, and Joel Despain at Crystal Cavern.

photo credits

Cover photos by Jon Kramer and Julie Martinez: Pluto's Cave (front main photo), Packsaddle Cave (back cover main photo), Black Chasm (back left inset), Eureka Mine (back middle inset), Lava Beds NM (back right inset)

All photos copyright Jon Kramer and Julie Martinez unless otherwise noted.

Sierra Nevada Recreation: 34 (bottom right), 35 (top) (bottom left) (bottom right), 36 (bottom left), 46 (bottom left), 132 (bottom), 133 (bottom left), 134 (top), (bottom right), 171 (top), (bottom right), 172 (top), (bottom right) **Sequoia Natural History Association:** 58 (bottom), 59 (top), (bottom left), (bottom right), 60 (top), (bottom left), (bottom right), 61 (top) **Eagle Mining Company:** 66, 68 (top), (bottom left), 69 (top) **Dave Bunnell:** 83, 84 (bottom), 85 (top),133 (top)

Artwork credits by artist and page number: **Vernon Morris**: 15 **Julie Martinez**: 19

Edited by Brett Ortler

Cover and book design by Jonathan Norberg

10 9 8 7 6 5 4 3 2 1

Copyright 2009 by Jon Kramer and Julie Martinez
Published by Adventure Publications, Inc.
820 Cleveland Street South
Cambridge, MN 55008
1-800-678-7006
www.adventurepublications.net
All rights reserved
Printed in China
ISBN-13: 978-1-59193-230-7
ISBN-10: 1-59193-230-0

Table of Contents

Welcome to the Underworld

In my senior year studying geology at the University of Maryland, I was expected, as all undergrads are, to adopt a Senior Research Project. The requirements were simple: The program must involve a problem-solving study directly related to one's chosen geology specialty. I had several passions in geology but a few stood out: excavating fossils and exploring caves. So I considered it natural to define a study which incorporated both. But when I proposed my project to the faculty board—comprised of die-hard ore petrologists and hard-rock stratigraphers—they thought I was joking. *Cave sedimentation? What the heck is that? Come-on Kramer, get serious* . . . The fact is these respected academic researchers had not the slightest clue what caves have to offer even though they were degreed geologists. It was time to teach the teachers.

The academic year went by quickly. In the course of 9 months I logged over 200 hours underground. *Where's Kramer? they'd ask. Oh, he's underground—probably down some rat hole or digging up catacombs* . . . I was in caves almost every weekend that year. On occasion I'd take an assistant or two, usually culled from our university geology club. Most of these neophytes had never been in a cave for real. Poor unwitting victims, they were subject to all manner of physical humiliation—crawling over shifting rubble, squirming through muddy tunnels, snaking through grimy squeezes, rappelling down cavernous drops, slogging through cold underground lakes. We dug test pits and lugged out hundreds of sample bags full of sediment. Deep inside labyrinthine caverns we ate squashed, muck-laden sandwiches with our grime-encrusted paws, and drank rancid coffee from mud-choked cups, all the while trying to sustain a body core temperature somewhat above that of a corpse. On the longer expeditions, we hauled in our sleeping bags and attempted some furtive shut-eye, an altogether strange and foreign experience deep inside a cave, I can tell you.

After all this self-flagellation, when we returned to the surface, sometimes after 2 days underground, we were exhausted beyond words. Not to mention dirty. Despite all that (or maybe because of it!), every single one of those who had labored with me through the arduous underground immediately volunteered for more. Back at campus we'd regale our fellow students with stories of cave pearls, 30-foot-long soda straws, long twisted columns, and other wonders of the underworld. During that time, enthusiasm for caves became so great that the geology club began regular weekend trips to West Virginia, Kentucky, and Tennessee.

In the spring I presented my paper—*The Source of Sediments at Indian Cave*—to an audience of some 45 students and faculty. Through a raucous maelstrom of improvised props, colorful slides, and combined audio enhancement, I either blessed them with brilliance or baffled them with BS (I'd prefer to think the former). One thing's certain—the audience was not bored. And it's safe to say thereafter none of them ever viewed caves in the same ho-hum manner that they once did. In the end I got a standing ovation from all the students and even some of the faculty—the rest of the academics remained seated. But even for those in their seats I'd done my job—they had a little education on how truly cool the underground world is.

Sometimes you feel like a dog with a head lamp. Sometimes you look like one too!

The point is, once you really take a close look at these underground wonders, you cannot help but develop a fondness for the subterranean. From the strange rare creatures that inhabit them to the magnificent formations that line their walls, caves are unique environments that call you back for more and more. Ever since I entered my first cave at age 12 I've had a natural curiosity about them and underground mines. It's something I've carried throughout my life. And despite the hundreds of holes in the ground I've been in, I am always amazed to find each new experience "down-under" as rewarding as the first.

I hope you will feel the same way. See ya down there!

Jon   Julie

Jon and Julie

Caving vs. Spelunking

When you visit Europe, you'll hear all manner of the term "spelunking." The British and Europeans coined the term and have held onto it. But here's a little linguistic advice for you: in America the sport is usually called "caving," not spelunking, so be warned that if you use the word

Sometimes it's better in winter. Hal Halvorson caving in the Minnesota deep freeze.

spelunking in talking about your underground adventures, you may raise an eyebrow or two.

Using this Guide

Plan Ahead

We've hiked all over California to check out every hole in the ground we can find. The result is this book which, in our humble opinion, represents the best underground adventures the state has to offer to the general public. It is not meant to be a complete list of every single cave, mine, and lava tube you can squirm into. But it is a good cross section of the best in each category.

Our purpose here is to give you a feeling for the sites we have included in this guide. Keep in mind that although these sites are pretty reliably in the same place from year to year, things change in their operation or management. As a result, the hours may not be what they were last year, or the length of the tour might be different, or the ice cream stand on the corner may have changed into a taco shop. Any number of things can happen over time, so we recommend that you always call ahead to make sure you know what's what, especially if you're planning your family vacation around it.

Skill Level

For quick reference we rate the overall degree of difficulty for each adventure. We use a loose system of 5 Skill Levels as a general guide to help you understand a site's potential difficulty and its degree of danger. This translates to how serious this particular undertaking can be in terms of safety and intensity for people of average ability. **Please note that these are arbitrary ratings to be used only as a general guideline.** Since each person's experience, background, and skills are different, and since things always change (even underground), don't take these ratings as gospel. You must decide for yourself if you are comfortable and skilled enough to safely undertake any of these adventures. The Skill Levels we use in this book are:

1 The simplest of underground adventures. A safe, guided tour along improved paths and walkways. Generally a horizontal pattern with limited steps and tight spots. Great for the whole family, seniors, and the disabled.

2 A bit more demanding. May be professionally guided or self-guided. Access is improved but probably includes many steps and tight squeezes. Still a family-friendly environment but may be challenging for seniors/the disabled.

3 No improved access. Moderately difficult. Likely to include hiking or scrambling over loose, rough terrain, through muddy depressions, and tight squeezes. Not recommended for seniors or the disabled.

4 Wild and unimproved cavity with difficult access and poten-tially severe conditions. May require path finding underground. Likely to include poor footing, dangerous drop-offs, exposure to rockfall, negotiating tight squeezes, potential flooding, etc. Guides are highly recommended. Not for the out of shape or those without underground experience.

5 Extreme conditions prevail. Difficult access with danger-ous, potentially fatal hazards in many places. Likely to require rope protection and other specialized caving skills. Experienced 3-D underground path-finding necessary. Do not attempt unless you are a proficient underground explorer or are guided by an experienced professional.

Underground Basics

Even in stabilized mines set up for visitors, it's often a good idea to wear hard hats. Jon and Julie in the groove at Eureka Mine in Death Valley.

It may sound redundant by the time you get to the section on Safety Underground, but since we want you to get the message loud and clear we're obliged to tell you: It is not our job here to teach you how to explore underground. But if you are headed into the noncommercial subterranean world—even explorations considered "mild" by caving standards—there are a few basics you should be aware of:

- Explore only places that are within your ability. Do some homework on the site you intend to visit before you go. Call them up and/or do a web search. If it's too advanced for your level of skill, either choose another site or hook up with a guide.

- Do not enter the underground alone. While you're down-under, travel as a group. If you get separated from your group, sit down, stay put, and let them find you.

- Always carry three separate sources of light per person and make sure each backup is easily reachable (like in your pocket). There is nothing more terrifying or dangerous than being without light.

- Dress appropriately for the particular place and outfit yourself with proper basic caving equipment: hard hat with head lamp, coveralls, boots, gloves, water bottle, first aid kit.

- Go to the bathroom before entering. Do not ever use a cavern, lava tube, or even a mine as your own personal toilet. If it is likely you may have to go while underground, you must carry it out and dispose of it properly on the surface. That includes both #1 and #2, so be prepared (bring a "pee bottle" and "doggie bags") if that's a possibility. You can laugh all you want but please follow this important rule.

- Carry a good supply of water. This is especially important if you're in a desert environment or at a hot, dry location like the Lava Beds National Monument.

- Tell someone where you are going and when you'll be back. Once you've told them, make sure you stick to the plan! In an emergency, how can anyone help if they don't know where you are?

Leave No Trace

The underworld is anything but boring. Each hole-in-the-ground has its own personality—its own dynamic ecosystem that's as unique as a fingerprint. But caves are especially sensitive, fragile places which need your help if they are to survive. It is no exaggeration to say that your mere presence in a cave can impact it, more so than any other environment. To use a fairly worn, calcified metaphor: Think of yourself as a bull in a china shop. Even if you consider yourself a compassionate, gentle bull, graceful in your movements, you cannot negotiate through the many aisles of fragile glassware without inflicting some form of damage.

The oft-quoted saying "Take nothing but pictures, leave nothing but footprints" originated as part of the caver's code of ethics. Today many cavers consider that only the starting point of proper conduct underground. A new mantra "Leave No Trace" has come to the fore. Basically it preaches just what it says—be gentle as you can in these places and try to leave no trace of your visit.

Safety Underground

Personal Safety

Please keep this in mind: **In this guide we do not attempt to teach you the techniques of underground exploration— it's not possible for us to convey serious aspects of such training in this book. You are responsible for your own safety.** Read the two previous sentences again and take the message to heart. Serious underground exploration is a skill that is only learned through experience. You need an experienced caver to show you the ropes. If you are so

Rappelling can be the ultimate in caving fun, so long as it's done safely.

inclined, you may join any one of the thousands of National Speleological Society clubs (called "grottoes" in the society vernacular) whose purpose is exploration and conservation of the nation's underground wonders. It will blow your mind what's down there!

Many of the explorations we describe here are commercial ventures with improved trails. On these tours you have little to worry about—you'll be monitored and assisted as you travel through the cave or mine system. Others—such as Sunny Jim Sea Cave, Subway Cave, and some in the Lava Beds National Monument— are somewhat improved with man-made features such as steps to assist you.

But some of the entries we include here—Natural Bridges, Jot Dean Ice Cave, and many in Lava Beds NM—are truly "wild" caves, unimproved locations where you must rely on your own skills and knowledge to both enjoy the experience safely and make as little impact as possible. Approach such places with caution and awareness. Allow me to share a fundamental piece of wisdom I use when teaching rock climbing and caving. It's one of my favorite sayings from Edward Whymper, a mountain-eer in the 1800s who was the first to summit the Matterhorn. He advises, *"Do nothing in haste. Look well to each step. And from the beginning, think what may be the end."* Pay attention and do just that. Don't go running off and gleefully slide down any hole in the ground without checking it out first.

Flash Floods

Be aware of the weather—you do not want to be caught inside a cave with rising water! George Hecht negotiating through close quarters in Florida's Catacombs Cave during a fossil research expedition.

If you're striking out into the land down-under, be sure to check the weather first. Many caves, mines and lava tubes are sus-ceptible to flooding. You do not want to be in one of them when it's pouring down rain outside. If it has rained recently or is scheduled to do so anywhere in the region, DO NOT enter a wild cave. This is serious, so take note of it. People have died by ignoring this simple warning.

Rockfalls

Most limestone caves are very sta-ble. You often hear the best place to be in an earthquake is inside an active limestone cavern. But talus caves, lava tubes, and mines are another thing altogether. They have not had the healing cement that cave formations provide in their more-popular counterparts. When traveling the underground, pay attention to where you are going. Go slowly, cautiously, and stay on established pathways. If there are

Don't let this happen to you, especially in a cave.

none, be sure to watch the walls and ceilings for signs of weak-ness or precariously loose rock piles and stay away from them. Remember these are dynamic environments—just because the roof has held up for 12,000 years does not mean it won't fall on your head, especially if you mess with a supporting pillar.

How Caves Form

Limestone and Marble Caves

There are a variety of ways in which caves form but there is a general blueprint used by the Great Architect when constructing **solution** caves of limestone and marble, including the vast majority of those which are commercialized. We'll play a little game here called *Let's-Make-A-Cave*.

The most popular caves are formation-filled limestone caverns. Lake Shasta Caverns is an example of one.

For the purposes of this game you are bestowed endless super powers. Now don't be a smart-aleck and attempt to abuse this privilege by abolishing taxation, making yourself President, or stealing all the candy in the Hershey chocolate factory—remember your powers are only useful for this game! The game begins at the **Giant Rock Pile** which you'll need to make first to get things started. The rock in question should be limestone or marble. You need lots of that stuff—so go out and get it and pile it up. Cover the whole neighborhood with it, even the whole state if you want! Just make sure it's hundreds or thousands of feet thick. For both of these rocks—limestone and marble—the predominant mineral in the matrix is calcite, a fairly soft material which is susceptible to reaction with a number of acids. That'll come in handy later on.

We move now into the **Faulting and Fracturing** area. Let's give that rock some shake-and-bake to move it around. Bring in the "Mountain Making Machine"—that ought to do it! Set its dial to somewhere between 4 (medium) and 10 (maximum). This'll either push the rocks up into mountains, or shove them down into valleys, however you wish. Being that your layers of rock are solid and thus fairly brittle, you'll end up with a lot of cracks running through it. But don't sweat it—that's exactly what you want. Some of these cracks will be gathered together in "fracture zones" often associated with faults. Now pick one of these zones for your cave. Go ahead, choose whichever one you want.

Now let's play with the **Water Table**. The object is to bring the water table approximately in line with one of the fracture zones you created in the last step. How do you do that? Well how about using something from the "Climate Change Toolbox?" You can adjust climate any number of ways, by pulling cards such as "Bring on an Ice Age" (lower water), or "Advance a Rainforest" (higher water). This handy tool allows for more or less rainfall as you wish so you can fine-tune the height of the water table relative to your chosen cave location. Remember you need to have the water table just barely covering the fracture zone where you want your cave to be.

Let's move on to the real fun—the **Acid Baths** part of the game. You have a number of acids at your disposal: carbonic acid, sulfuric acid, acetic acid, etc. So how do we make the acids? Well you needn't worry, it all comes naturally just by playing with the "Environmental Effects" tools. Pump some CO_2 into the air, let it rain and presto! you have mild carbonic acid. How about putting some unstable pyrite in the rock layers above your cave? Once the rainwater percolates through that, it'll pick up some of the sulfur it needs and viola! there's sulfuric acid to throw in. Once you've adjusted the acids then you can introduce them into the water which is bathing your fracture zone.

Remember earlier when I said that calcium is susceptible to acids? Now you've really got the process going. The acids in the water from the previous step will attack the rock as they slowly move through the fractures, gradually dissolving the walls. But it takes time. Now all we have to do is put the whole thing in the closet for awhile and set the timer to anywhere from a few hundred thousand to several million years. When you come back later you see your fracture zone has now become a lot of hollowed-out regions in the rock. Perfect for a cavern!

Last step—go to the **Speleothem Decorations** box and select the cave formations you wish to have line the inside of your cave. Pin them up however you wish but follow the directions (please DO NOT put stalactites on the floor or stalagmites on the ceiling). Last, but not least, set the master dial to Active or Inactive depending on whether you want more formations in the future. Congratulations, you just made a cave; now open it up for tours!

Lava Tubes and Ice Caves

California volcanoes have provided an endless supply of underground adventures in the form of lava tubes.

It's a little different for lava tubes. But it's easier and faster than limestone caves. First, figure out where you want your lava tube cave to be and then introduce a volcano or two. They need not be huge, Hawaii-style volcanoes, but you do want them to erupt with rivers of lava, which run down their flanks and through nearby valleys. The top, sides, and bottom of these flows cool and solidify first, creating a tubular crust surrounding the flow with the still-molten lava inside continuing to move freely, like a river in a tunnel. However, once you turn off the spigot of magma, the liquid lava inside empties out, leaving behind hollow lava tube caves. Simple as that. Now go do it.

Oh, by the way, to make an ice cave all you need to do is find a suitable lava tube which is well insulated and situate it at a high enough elevation and latitude to accumulate a lot of ice. Turn the ice machine on in the winter and off in the summer. If you've picked the right location, you should have ice year-round!

A Brief History of the California Underworld

It's no secret that prehistoric Indians used caves for shelter, burials, and rituals. In Europe, some of the famous cave paintings of France and Spain are older than 30,000 years, attesting to the great longevity of cavern use by humans. In North America things are quite a bit younger, probably because people colonized this continent much later. Thus far we have only scant evidence of humans here predating 15,000 years, although some researchers argue populations entered North America some tens of thousands of years prior. As in other parts of the prehistoric world, some of the earliest evidence of humans in North America has been found in cave deposits. As I showed in my own undergrad research, caves are virtual time capsules. Excavating a cave's sediments is like turning pages in a book—each cave yields different parts of the story.

Native peoples have utilized California caves for thousands of years. Chumash Cave is an example of one such cave.

It's not easy to say when the first cave was discovered in California or by whom. Undoubtedly it was by Native Americans who had several good reasons for finding and using them. Caves offer natural shelters with built-in climate control. Dry caves also offer protection for grain and storage of goods. Many caves are a source of clean water. In several places early inhabitants left deliberate evidence of their stay in the form of petroglyphs and pictographs (rock carvings and rock paintings), some of which are associated with caves. But because we cannot talk with those who made them, these symbols and impressions give us only a slight glimpse into the world of these early Americans.

Not much is written about American caves before the nineteenth century, likely due to the fact most people here were just caught up in the tasks of everyday life. Even so, some people were making a pretty good living because of caves: Mining of cave deposits—a major source of saltpeter (potassium nitrate), the primary ingredient in gunpowder—fueled the American Revolution and the War Between the States. By the mid-1800s, even before the California Gold Rush, the American public was hearing reports of huge, expansive caverns that boggled the mind.

Until the early 1800s California was strictly a wilderness territory reached mainly by boat, and then only along the coast. Nevertheless, most of the state's caves are far inland, along the Sierras, and thus out of reach from the coastal communities. So it's no wonder that the first whites to see the splendors of the California underground were prospectors who braved

Although relatively new on the scene, European immigrants recognized a good thing when they saw it. The Inscription Room at California Caverns.

the wilderness and took off for the hills in search of California's famous gold. The first solid evidence we have of an Anglo connection in the state's caves is at California Cavern where the earliest names date, not surprisingly, from 1849, the year of the California Gold Rush. California Cavern, located in the heart of gold country, became quickly famous and served as a regional stopping point for those passing through the area. One might say it was California's original tourist attraction. One telling inscription recorded by a group out for a midday visit declares: "Lunch 11 am, July 24th, 1881 . . . " followed by the signatures of the party. Hundreds of other signatures and inscriptions line a few of the chambers in what was called at the time "Mammoth Cavern." There's even one from the WW II era that reads "Kilroy was here, Sept 2, 1946." You are welcome to visit California Cavern and see them for yourself. Tell them we sent you.

Map of Sites

1

Alabama Hills

type of site: eroded granite with natural cavities, tunnels and arches

skill level: 2–3

equipment needed: sturdy hiking shoes, water and a camera

temperature: influenced by ambient temperatures

tour length: it's all about you, so spend a few hours or all day

description: The formations here are not comparable in size to, say, Arches National Monument, but they are far more numerous and a lot more accessible. These hills are a delight for anyone and everyone who has a kid inside them clamoring to get out. You can't help but enjoy roaming the channels, ridges, spires and small canyons looking for new surprises. And you'll find plenty! There are arches, bridges, tunnels, small caves, and cavities scattered all over the place. There are arches on arches and hollows in hollows. There are double, triple and even quadruple-chambered cavities. There are rocks that are empty and look like giant egg shells. I really cannot even begin to describe all the weird and wonderful things here so please just go check it out for yourself! While you're at it, continue on up to Whitney Portal and see the splendor that is the highest mountain in the lower 48 states, Mt. Whitney.

directions: From Lone Pine, follow the Whitney Portal Road west toward Mt. Whitney for 2.7 miles. Turn right (north) onto Movie Road (aka Movie Flat Road). This tract starts as fairly decent pavement but gradually degrades to a dirt road in about half a mile. Follow the road about 1.5 miles from Whitney Portal Road to a "Y." Bear right here and pull into the parking area immediately on your left. The trail to the most popular arch is clearly marked. But don't ignore all the rest of the hills in the immediate area—there are surprises around every corner.

precautions: The granite here is continually weathering and crumbling—so watch your footing. The loose grit will pull your feet right out from under you if you aren't careful. In addition, this is rattlesnake country—please don't put your hands anywhere you haven't first inspected. You might surprise yourself and a snake too. Avoid midsummer heat and carry lots of water whenever you go.

geology

Have you ever been to Joshua Tree National Monument? If you haven't, you won't know what I mean when I say the geology of this place will remind you of it. (So get on over to Josh and study up on it.) These hills hiding below the eye of Mt. Whitney and its neighbors are composed of fine-to-medium grained granite that has decided to divest itself of itself. That is, the material is so poorly cemented that it's in a constant state of decay—weathering itself into oblivion. The elements attack with vigor, but some sections of granite hold up better than others, resulting in the plethora of holes you'll find here.

history

You probably were wondering as you drove through Lone Pine what all the hoopla was about with the movie this, the movie that, and the Movie Museum, and Movie Road, and Movie Flat Tours, etc., etc. . . . Well, it so happens that there were more than a few motion pictures (mostly westerns) shot on location here. If you visit the Movie Museum in town you'll find a whole long list of them, along with memorabilia and posters from many. The town has been an out-of-the-way favorite among Hollywood tycoons for several decades and still welcomes the folks from Tinseltown whenever the need arises.

The Alabama Hills and its wild formations sit just below the watchful eye of Mt. Whitney and her friends. There are several places one can photo-frame the mountains through an arch.

The wild rock formations here are a result of spheroidal weathering *(weathering of rocks which continually rounds off its edges, ultimately resulting in semi-spherical shapes) working in diabolical ways to attack the mostly-vertical cracks and fractures.*

ABOVE: *Many arches here make it easy to naturally frame whomever you'd like.*

RIGHT: *There's holy and there's holey. And then there's this place, holy holey!*

ABOVE: *At first glance they look like fossilized pods left over from the* Invasion of the Body Snatchers. *But they're probably not.*

BELOW: *There's got to be a name for the kind of formation where you can stick your feet out of one cave and your head out of another.*

RIGHT: *Hey, isn't that Paul Bunyan's schnoz over there?*

How many arches can you find to frame Mt. Whitney and the mountains nearby? This kind of photo-op is so abundant that it gets to be kind of kitschy. Almost, but not really.

IF YOU GO . . .

contact info: Bishop Field Office, phone: (760) 872-5000;
   www.blm.gov/ca/st/en/fo/bishop/scenic_byways/alabamas.html
fee: no fee
hours: always open, but it's best to stick to daytime
lodging: several campgrounds along Whitney Portal Road; lodging
   in Lone Pine
aboveground: plenty of hiking and scenery; climb to the top of Mt. Whitney

2

Black Chasm Cavern

type of site: active limestone cavern, mostly vertical

skill level: 2

equipment needed: nothing other than common sense and a camera

temperature: constant 57°F

tour length: guided walking tour usually runs about 50 minutes

description: At first, the tour through Black Chasm Cavern is anything but spectacular. Getting "down in" isn't so different than dozens of other caves and the formations you encounter are pretty typical speleothems (cave formations) similar to those found in most garden-variety caverns. But even in the early stages of the tour, you start to see signs that this is not your typical home-grown cave system. Helictites, which are strange, gravity-defying cave formations, peek out from small cracks and crevices. To the untrained eye this isn't a big deal. But for those of us "in the under-ground," this is a tantalizing suggestion that even more interesting spe-leothems are nearby; indeed, at the last stop you are rewarded with one of the most spectacular displays in the subterranean world. The Landmark Room is home to the most incredible helictite formations you will ever see outside of Lechuguilla, which is *the* place for helictites and is located in Carlsbad Caverns National Park in New Mexico. And since you are not likely to be one of the exceptionally few people allowed in Lechuguilla (which is closed for its protection), this is the place to go to see these rare and wondrous formations.

directions: From Stockton, take Highway 88 east to Jackson. Turn left at the lights to continue on Highway 88 east to Pine Grove. Make a left turn toward Volcano on Pine Grove-Volcano Road and continue about 2.5 miles to the bottom of the steep hill. Make a sharp right turn onto Pioneer-Volcano Road and continue about 1,500 feet. Turn right at the Black Chasm National Natural Landmark entrance.

precautions: This is a commercial cavern with improved walkways, steps and railings. The management advises not to carry small children in backpacks. Front packs are OK so long as you are careful in areas with low ceilings.

geology

What's up with helictites, those strange formations that grow at odd angles? For crying out loud, don't they know about gravity? Unlike most cave formations, which grow in response to gravity, helictites are not typical speleothems (cave formations). The exact mechanics of helictite formation are not well understood and there are many theories that attempt to explain how they form. Just when someone thinks they have the key, along comes a helictite that blows away their theory. We do know that helictites, like many formations, are composed of calcite and/or aragonite, two common components of many cave formations. The fact is, helictites defy simple explanation. Isn't it nice when we discover we don't know everything?!

history

It's no surprise the original cavern tours were confined to the regions of the first several rooms, as they were the easiest to access. But, in later years, as various parties pushed the mapped limits of Black Chasm farther and farther, some intrepid cavers broke through to the Landmark Room and found what was instantly recognized as one of the true gems of the American underground—a pristine collection of amazing helictites in a dizzying array of shapes and sizes. It's a rarity that earned Black Chasm Cavern the distinction of National Natural Landmark in 1976.

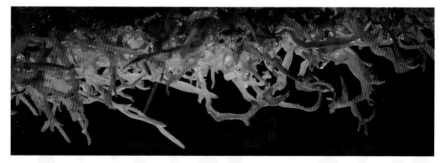

It's alive! It's alive! Well . . . kind of, in a speleological sort of way. Helictites doing their thing.

Although known for its incredible abundance of helictites, Black Chasm also has its fair share of good old stalactites.

ABOVE: *An abundance of stalactites conspiring together to form a drapery.*

RIGHT: *Cave bacon is not as tasty as the porcine variety but not as smelly either.*

ABOVE: *They're wild! You will not find a better collection of gravity-defying helictites open to the public in North America.*

RIGHT: *The entrance is a series of steps down into the abyss.*

In defiance of its own name, the colors in Black Chasm Cavern span the rainbow. One of the extensive calcite draperies in mid-tour.

IF YOU GO . . .

contact info: Black Chasm Cavern, phone: 866-762-2837; www.caverntours.com/blackdir.htm

fee: per-person fee; group rates available

hours: open every day; tour times vary with season

lodging: camping at Chaw'se Indian Grinding Rock State Park; lodging in Jackson

aboveground: gemstone mining, gold panning, geode cracking, nature trail, picnic area with tables, new 3,000-square-foot visitor center/gift shop

3

Boyden Cavern

type of site: active limestone cavern

skill level: 2

equipment needed: none for the walking tour; you will be provided equipment and instruction for the aboveground canyoneering and rappelling adventures

temperature: constant 55°F

tour length: guided walking tour is approximately 45 minutes; canyoneering and rappelling tours are either a ½ day or a full day and tailored to your experience, interests and personal agenda

description: If the setting were any more exotic you'd think you were in a foreign country. Well, in fact, for a little while during the tour underground, maybe you are! Boyden Cavern is located in Kings Canyon inside Sequoia National Monument beneath the massive, 2,000-foot-high marble walls of the famous Kings Gates. If you've never been to this park, then you don't know what you're missing. But I'm here to tell you it's one of the great natural wonders of California. Just the scenery around this cavern is worth the trip. The popular 45-minute walking tour is suitable for the entire family, from kids to senior citizens. It begins with a steep, five-minute walk to the cavern entrance; from there, visitors travel deep within, but don't worry—groups follow a well-lit and handrail-equipped trail as guides point out many natural varieties of formations.

directions: From Fresno, take Highway 180 east into Kings Canyon National Park. Follow Highway 180 east into the canyon approximately 16 miles past Grant Grove Village and the Kings Canyon Visitor Center. At the very bottom of the canyon the road crosses the Kings River for the first time. The cavern parking lot is just off the road on your right before the bridge.

precautions: This is a commercial cavern with improved walkways, steps and railings. The management advises not to carry small children in backpacks. Front packs are OK so long as you are careful in the area of low ceilings.

geology

Boyden Cavern is not as loaded with cave formations as other caves, but it serves up the standard fare of stalactites, stalagmites, columns, and soda straws. The cavern geology is even more compelling than the cave formations. Boyden is situated at the intersection of rocks with differing lithologies (types of rock strata), which complicates the geologic interpretation. Its passages formed inside a large marble complex called the Boyden Cavern Roof Pendant, which was once a limestone "roof" over a granite batholith (a giant "bubble" of magma which hardens below the surface). The limestone formed in shallow seas long before the Sierra Nevada was pushed up into a mountain range, a process which began only a few million years ago and is still happening.

Although originally discovered by a survey crew in the 1800s, it was Putnam Boyden (on the right) who acquired the rights, secured the entrance, and offered the first tours in 1907. By the looks of it, he and his friends were well armed and didn't mess around with trespassers—"Pay up, or else!"

Boyden is not known as a place with a huge abundance of cave formations. But what it does have is pretty cool.

ABOVE: *A stalagmite that's trying mighty hard to become a column.*

RIGHT: *Cascading stalagmites and draperies.*

ABOVE: *The tour here is a fun trip that gets you up-close and personal with the formations. Be sure to take the option of the "natural exit" if it's available.*

RIGHT: *The short hike to the entrance follows the river.*

BELOW: *The setting here is really incredible.*

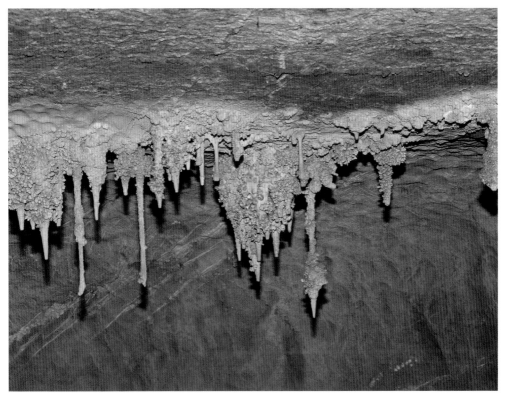

Some of the weirder speleothems in Boyden are these ornate soda straw formations.

IF YOU GO . . .

contact info: Boyden Cavern, phone: (559) 338-0959; www.caverntours.com/BoydenRt.htm

fee: per-person fee; group rates available; NOTE: To reach this cavern you must drive into Sequoia and Kings Canyon National Park which charges a per-vehicle entrance fee (good for 7 days); this fee is NOT associated with Boyden Cavern; you must pay an additional fee to tour the caverns

hours: open April to November depending on snowfall and access; closed January, February, and March; tour times vary with season

lodging: camping and lodging in Sequoia and Kings Canyon National Park

aboveground: Boyden Caverns also leads supremely cool aboveground canyoneering and rappelling trips; if you haven't been on one, you're missing out; these are by advance reservation only

4

Bronson Cave

type of site: excavated tunnel complex in an old quarry; famous historic filming location

skill level: 1.5

equipment needed: a flashlight is advisable

temperature: influenced by ambient temperatures

tour length: you're on your own here—1 hour or more

description: In a stroke of geographical genius, someone in the county cartography department named Bronson Cave for Bronson Canyon where it resides. The "cave," such as it is, is actually not a cave at all. Instead, it's a machine-made branching tunnel system carved through the ridge by a local stone company, probably prior to 1925. As you enter the site from the dirt road, you'll notice the main tunnel entrance on your right. Upon entering you can easily see through to the other side (assuming you are here in the daytime!) some 100 yards away. As you head that direction you'll encounter two branchings off the main tunnel, each with its own exit out the other end. It's interesting to note that the famed Hollywood sign is not visible on your hike to the quarry and into the main tunnel entrance. However, when you exit the other side, look up and to the left. There, in all its glory, is the omnipresent monument looming like Big Brother.

directions: This site is located in Griffith Park in Los Angeles. From US 101 head east on Franklin Ave. approximately 0.8 miles to Bronson Ave.. Set your odometer to 0.0 here and head north on Bronson. At 0.4 miles you will merge with Canyon Dr. At 1.0 miles you will enter the park through the old gates. At 1.3 miles you will come to a locked gate with a small parking area just to your left. The foot trail to the cave is a gated access road across the street from the parking area and a little bit south. Follow this dirt road uphill about 0.25 miles where the road bends to the right. The tunnel entrance is to your left.

precautions: The road to the tunnels and the tunnels themselves are very easy and safe. But be careful of following any paths beyond this area. Some of them run along dangerous cliff edges with deadly drop-offs. Also do not leave your car unattended after dark. The neighborhood is rather unsavory. Break-ins have occurred here.

geology

The Bronson "caves," such as they are, have been hollowed out of a hill on the western side of Griffith Park. Actually they are not caves at all, but quarry tunnels left behind by the Union Rock Company which mined the local metamorphic rock for use as aggregate in the early 1900s. You have to admit that the near-downtown location had to have been pretty handy when supplying crushed stone to city road crews who were busy paving the area. The quarry was active for nearly two decades and was finally abandoned around 1928. About that time Batman was looking for a new Bat Cave and guess what happened next . . .

history

OK, admit it—ever since the first time you saw the opening scenes of Batman, you've always dreamt of a ride in the Batmobile. And although that's not likely to happen, you can visit the actual spot where that scene was filmed, thereby fulfilling at least part of the fantasy. This old abandoned rock quarry and its "caves" are one of Hollywood's most famous filming locations. Easily accessed, Bronson Canyon has had thousands of scenes filmed here, including many in the Batman series. Some locals even refer to the place as "Batman Cave."

Batman used this place to park the Batmobile.

It may not be a natural cave, but at least you can see the Hollywood sign from here!

IF YOU GO . . .

contact info: Griffith Park Headquarters, phone: 323-913-4688

fee: no fee; if you live nearby, why not become a park volunteer? If you're not from here then you can make a donation at the zoo, which is also located in Griffith Park

hours: open daily whenever the park is open

lodging: improved camping and lodging in Los Angeles

aboveground: this is the "Central Park" of L.A.; all the rest of Griffith Park awaits you, including the zoo

5

California Cavern

type of site: active horizontal limestone cave complex

skill level: 1.5 for the standard walking tours, 3 for the expeditions

equipment needed: a jacket and a good camera are about all you need on the regular walking tours; on the expeditions you are provided with a hard hat, lamps, gloves, coveralls and you'll be briefed on the conditions and what else you should bring

temperature: constant 55 degrees year-round

tour length: the *Trail of Lights* and the *Trail of Lakes* are family-oriented walking tours that run about 60–80 minutes; the *Mammoth Cave Expedition* is 2–3 hours; the *Middle Earth Expedition* is up to 4 hours

description: There are not many places in North America that can compare with California Cavern, where impressive geology, prehistoric fossils, ancient Indian culture and the legendary '49ers are all featured in a unique and rewarding underground experience. The management, led by the knowledgeable and affable John Fairchild, has done an admirable job of offering up one of the best cavern adventures this side of the Mississippi. There are two main walking tours—the *Trail of Lakes* and the *Trail of Lights* —both are approximately 60–80 minutes long, and experienced, profession- al guides lead the way into such places as the recently discovered "Jungle Room," named for the array of crystalline "vines" covering the ceiling, many of them several feet long. And then there are the expeditions: the *Middle Earth Expedition* and the *Mammoth Cave Expedition* for those who want to "get down and dirty" with a real caving experience.

directions: From Stockton take Highway 4 east to Angels Camp, then Highway 49 north to San Andreas. Turn right on Mountain Ranch Road and drive approximately 9 miles. Turn right at the 2nd Michel Road turnoff and the California Historical Landmark sign that says "California Caverns." Follow the signs for approximately 2 miles to the driveway on the left.

precautions: This is a commercial cavern with improved walkways, steps and railings. On the expeditions you must be physically fit and willing to endure standard caving situations; be prepared to get very muddy, crawl through tunnels and negotiate rough, slippery terrain.

geology

It's another day of cave construction here in the Calaveras Complex. The Calaveras Complex originally consisted of sedimentary deposits of limestone and shale that were laid down some 250 million years ago in a shallow sea. Later, the layers were compressed. Because of the Sierra Nevada Uplift (an on-going tectonic process which is increasing the elevation of the mountains) groundwater seeps through the rock and is carving out many holes in the easily-eroded marble, producing many caves. Several of these caves are open to the public; Moaning Cavern, Mercer Cavern, and Natural Bridges are among them.

history

Native Americans used California Cavern for perhaps thousands of years but when, exactly, it was discovered by westerners is a matter of some controversy. Apparently somebody got their dates mixed up way-back-when and so all we can gather is it was either in 1849 or 1850. No matter, what we do know is the discovery was made by one Captain Joseph Taylor who, while out target practicing one day, noticed a breeze emanating from some nearby rocks. Upon investigating this curious phenomenon, Taylor discovered the entrance to the cave.

During most of the year, the bottom part of California Cavern lies under a crystal-clear lake.

Is it possible to have an overabundance of cave formations? If so, this place probably does.

ABOVE: *The '49ers left their mark along with hundreds of others who visited here. The Inscription Room is wall-to-wall signatures. But don't even think of carving your own initials here—it's against the law and that's a good thing.*

RIGHT: *Some of the formations here are pretty strange, and that's a good reason to visit this place.*

ABOVE: *Stalactites and soda straws hang from the roof.*

RIGHT: *Stalagmites climb up from the floor.*

BELOW: *The array of beautiful colors mixes with an endless variety of formations throughout the cavern.*

I have a fascination with soda straws and this is one place where I can indulge my appetite for them.

IF YOU GO . . .

contact info: California Cavern, phone: 866-762-2837;
www.caverntours.com/CalifRt.htm

fee: per-person fee; group rates available; expeditions require
advance reservations

hours: open every day; tour times vary with season

lodging: incredible camping at Calaveras Big Trees State Park; lodging in
Murphys and Angels Camp

aboveground: gemstone mining, gold panning, geode cracking, nature trail,
picnic area with tables and new visitor center/gift shop

California State Mining and Mineral Museum

type of site: re-created underground gold mine with an adjacent museum which houses the official California state mineral collection

skill level: 1

equipment needed: none, but bring the camera!

temperature: buildings are climate-controlled

tour length: self-guided, 1 hour or more

description: OK, so it's technically not a real underground mine or cavern. And, yes, the mine shaft here is sort-of make-believe. But the artifacts are all real, presented in a realistic manner, and housed in a realistic setting. It may not be a real mine, but it's the next best thing, as it's far more educational and a lot safer. As a result, it's a great place to take the kids anytime of year. There's plenty for adults too, even if you're not that moved by geology or the intricacies of asymmetric amalgams in the assay office. There are plenty of hands-on educational aspects encompassing all aspects of mining—not just gold.

directions: Located at the Mariposa County Fairgrounds. Follow Highway 49 about 1.8 miles south of Mariposa. Turn left into fairgrounds and into the parking lot. Follow the signs.

precautions: Beware! The rocks on display here will tempt you. Some of the finest law-abiding, tax-paying citizenry of America have fantasized about absconding with a few of the state's fine mineral specimens, especially those of the gold variety. But keep this in mind—crime doesn't pay and we assume no responsibility for your actions.

geology

All minerals, under ideal conditions, form as crystals, which occur in various shapes, sizes and configurations. But those of the more malleable variety—copper, gold, etc.—tend to be crushed by the movement of the rocks in which they formed. That's why crystals of these varieties are rare. And then there's the fact that people are not inclined to keep such crystalline specimens intact for the simple reason that they don't want or need a display ornament. It's more about, "Melt it down and show me the money!" So it's a real treat for crystal nuts the world over when someone goes the extra mile, forgoes the immediate payoff, and preserves such a rare piece. On display here is one such prize: the famous Fricot "Nugget," a rare and beautiful specimen of crystallized gold discovered in the American River in 1864. This spectacular, 13.8-pound specimen is the largest remaining intact mass of crystalline gold from nineteenth century California.

history

The entire region, not surprisingly, is rich with history, especially that which relates to the precious yellow metal. This is the area in which explorers John C. Fremont and Kit Carson found the rich Mariposa Vein and opened the first mill to crush ore and extract gold in California. You are invited to discover for yourself California's mineral wealth, colorful history and geologic diversity at this educational stop along the famous Gold Trail of Route 49.

SERPENTINE
(California's State Rock)
This metamorphic rock formed when sedimentary rocks were chemically and physically changed by very hot, mineral-rich fluids that rose from...

Although minerals are the backbone of mining and other industries, they are little respected by most folks. Not so here, where they display much of the official state mineral collection. Serpentine (left) and borax (right).

Gold is such a soft mineral that it rarely forms crystals. But given the right conditions it forms beautiful crystal clusters such as this one.

IF YOU GO . . .

contact info: museum information, phone: (209) 742-7625;
   www.parks.ca.gov/?page_id=588
fee: per-person fee, group rates available; educational tours booked in
   advance are FREE
hours: open every day; hours vary seasonally
lodging: improved camping and lodging in Mariposa
aboveground: you're not too far from Yosemite and if you can't find something
   to do there, then you may as well find a roundhouse and sit in the corner

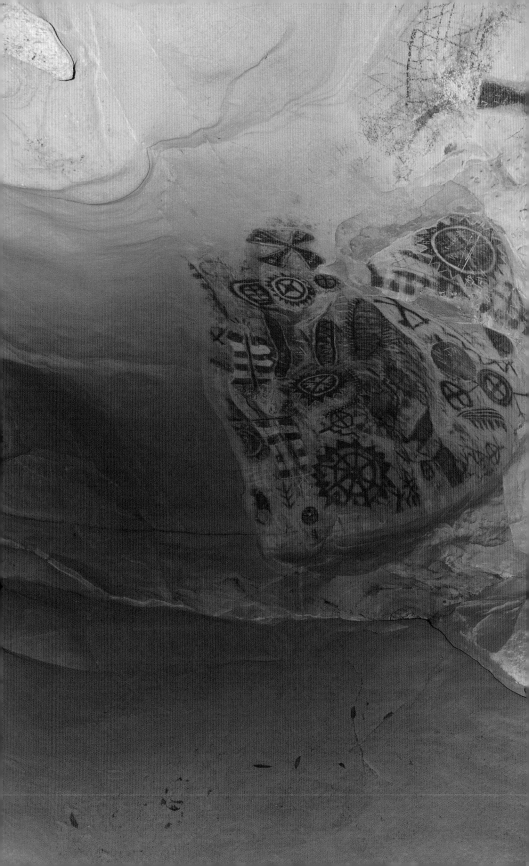

7

Chumash Painted Cave

type of site: small, dry cave shelter and archaeological site

skill level: 1

equipment needed: nothing but a camera

temperature: ambient

tour length: self-guided, less than 1 hour

description: Chumash Painted Cave suffers from an identity crisis. It's not much in the way of a cave, and what little cave there is has been gated off, so you cannot enter it. And then there's the lack of any *bona fide* parking area anywhere at all. Yet it is under the protection of the California State Park system, although you'd not know it except for a little sign in front. So what gives—why list it in our book as if it was some form of adventure? Well, for one thing it's among the best, most well-preserved Native American cave pictograph sites in the country and probably the only one you'll get a chance to see up close. Despite the locked gate, you can easily see into the cave and view the colorful art lining its walls.

The experience is reminiscent of the famous Paleolithic cave paintings of France and Spain, only you don't have to do all that traveling overseas (assuming you would be let into one of those caves, which is not likely to happen). It's a pretty cool place with some incredible artwork on the walls, so if you are in the area, we recommend you stop by. You'll be glad you did.

directions: The site is three miles south of the San Marcos Pass. Take Highway 154 out of Santa Barbara and turn right on Painted Caves Road. The cave is located on the left, about two miles from the turn, up a steep, narrow road. The pullout at the site will only accommodate one or two vehicles so parking might be a little tricky.

precautions: Pay attention while you're driving up here. The road is narrow and winding and has an affinity for car accidents. Don't try taking a big RV up here!

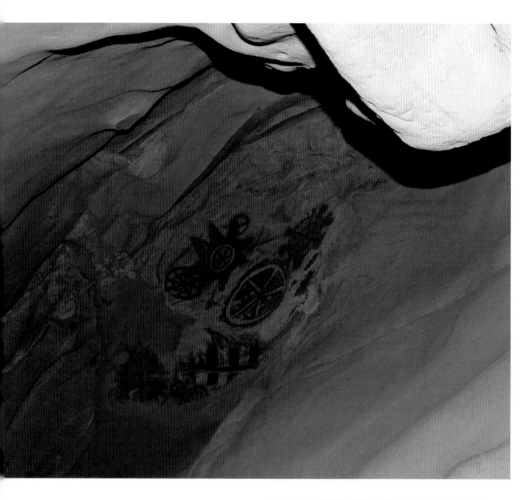

ABOVE: *There are very few pictographs in North America which are preserved in such an excellent condition.*

RIGHT: *More examples of the wonderful pictographs here.*

BELOW: *When you see this sign, quit driving —you're here!*

The cave is located in a hollowed-out fissure produced by selective weathering of the sandstone. Here's evidence of it at the cave entrance.

IF YOU GO . . .

contact info: Chumash Painted Cave State Historic Park, telephone: (805) 733-3713; www.parks.ca.gov/?page_id=602

fee: no fee, but, hey, you're no slouch and eager to donate a few greenbacks to help the cause, so why not make a donation to *The Archaeological Conservancy* 5301 Central Avenue NE, Suite 902, Albuquerque, NM, 87108-1517; phone: (505) 266-1540

hours: daylight hours

lodging: camping and lodging both nearby in Santa Barbara

aboveground: well, there are nice views on a clear day but not much else you can do here except dodge cars on the narrow road

8

Crystal Cave

type of site: active horizontal limestone cave complex

skill level: 1 for *Regular Tour* and *Discovery Tour*, 3.5 for *Wild Cave Tour*

equipment needed: because of the constant cool temperature down under, you'll need a jacket and warm clothes; the *Wild Cave Tour* folks supply all other necessary caving gear (hard hat, gloves, kneepads, etc.)

temperature: constant 48 degrees, year-round

tour length: the *Regular Tour* is 45 minutes, the *Discovery Tour* is 1½–2 hours, and the *Wild Cave Tour* is 4–6 hours

description: Get this straight: Anyone wishing to visit Crystal Cave must be part of a guided tour. *But there's a catch—tour tickets are not sold at the cave entrance. They must be purchased in person at the Foothills or Lodgepole visitor centers in Sequoia National Park.* After purchasing tickets, allow at least 1½ hours to arrive at the cave. So make sure you plan this right or you'll be sitting in a parking lot imagining what's underground about half a mile down the path. In all cases you meet your guide at the "Spider Web Gate," the official entrance to the cave. On the *Regular Tour* you're served up a healthy fare of creatively-named speleothems and rock features in an underground geological smorgasbord. Beautiful stalactites, stalagmites, and curtains crowd impressively large cavities. Ornate marble walls naturally polished by a subterranean stream make for a nice geologic dessert after a filling meal of underground delights. The *Discovery Tour* is a popular 1½-hour trip with a more in-depth experience in smaller groups. It provides a deeper understanding of the geology and wildlife of the cave environment. And for the intrepid caver, there's the 4–6 hour *Wild Cave Tour* that gets you good and dirty.

directions: Crystal Cave is located off the Generals Highway in Sequoia National Park, between the Ash Mountain entrance and Giant Forest. To reach the cave, turn west onto Crystal Cave Road (paved) and follow it to the end at the cave parking lot. From here the cave entrance is about a half-mile hike along the main path. Note: No vehicles longer than 22 feet are allowed on Crystal Cave Road.

precautions: Although the trails inside are paved, the cave is not wheelchair accessible. Also—no tripods, walking sticks, strollers, or baby backpacks are allowed in the cave. Canes, if used for mobility, are allowed.

geology

Sinking Streams—Crystal Cave is a classic example of a "sinking-stream cavern" where the dominant force in formation of this world underground is flowing water. At one time this level was filled with water and the stream here flowed through the strata above, helping to form the cave systems in the upper layers. As the stream carved its way down, these eventually became Bear Den Cave, Phosphorescent Room, Pool Room, Dome Room and other passages which abide above. Ultimately the stream carved down to the point where the tours are held today—Marble Hall, Junction Room, and Spider Web Gate areas. If we wait around long enough there'll be even more rooms to explore as the stream carves out more of the marble sediments below. But don't hold your breath, that could take a few million years.

history

It's hard to imagine in this day and age of Geologic Enlightenment that our race still harbors vandals, but it's true. In 2003 vandals destroyed hundreds of formations in three caves in Sequoia National Park, including several in the entranceway to Crystal Cave. In response, the Sequoia Natural History Association created the **Protect Sequoia Caves Program** to raise awareness about cave conservation and protection of these and other natural resources in the national parks. Basically you buy a nifty little button to show your support. Proceeds from the sale of this button go directly to this effort. So, what are you waiting for? Go ahead and do it!

For a real caving adventure, grab your hard hat (or borrow one from the guides) and crawl around in the mud with the Wild Cave Tour, a 4–6 hour true geological experience.

There are many reasons why this cave is the most popular one in California. Here are just a few.

ABOVE: *Does anyone have an idea why the entryway is called the Spider Web Gate? I guess you'll just have to take the tour to find out.*

RIGHT: *Lots of room and lots of incredible formations. The walking tour follows an improved walkway.*

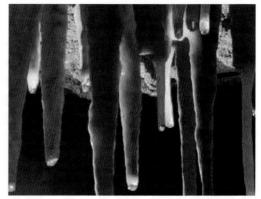

ABOVE: *Gigantic stalagmites are all over in the underground.*

BELOW: *It goes on and on, but the 45 minutes passes way too quickly.*

RIGHT: *This is an active cave system that is still building formations. Here thin stalactites do their best to start a soda straw factory.*

Another fine example of the type of the speleothems you'll find here.

IF YOU GO . . .

contact info: Sequoia Natural History Association, phone: (559) 565-3759; www.sequoiahistory.org/cave/cave.htm

fee: per-person fee; NOTE: Tour tickets are not sold at the cave entrance and must be purchased in person at the Foothills/Lodgepole visitor centers in Sequoia National Park; after purchasing tickets, allow at least 1$\frac{1}{2}$ hours before going to the cave

hours: open daily mid May–mid October; hours vary with season

lodging: camping inside the park; lodging at Wuksachi Village

aboveground: some of the best hiking in the state is nearby

9

Dublin Gultch

type of site: historic excavated living and storage chambers carved into cliffs of volcanic ash

skill level: 1.5

equipment needed: wear decent boots—this is snake country; don't forget to use sunscreen

temperature: most of this site is aboveground and outside, so whatever the weather is, you're stuck with it

tour length: self-guided, stay at least an hour or two

description: Well, they're not really caves, but they are pretty neat and they are underground—or in the ground, as the case may be. The idea to carve homes into the soft igneous rock no doubt originated with people who sought refuge from the intense summer heat. They did so by ducking into the natural cavities that pepper this area. It's not really known who were the first people to set up subterranean housekeeping here, but by the late 1800s, Dublin Gultch was a full-on boomtown. Carving out the chambers was certainly no picnic, but it was a lot easier than digging into the harder rocks which make up most of the solid mountains of the area. Several folks lived underground here, apparently rent-free, and many of the homes were outfitted with solid doors, windows, and even wood-burning stoves for heat in the winter. Several original stove pipes still hail from the hilltops. The last residents left in the 1960s.

directions: Dublin Gultch is at Shoshone. Access to the area is via a dirt tract south of town on the west side of route 127 just before route 178 branches off to the east. It is marked with a sign. The area is also called the "Dublin Caves."

precautions: The place can be blazing hot in the summer months so dress accordingly and wear sunscreen. Also carry plenty of water.

geology

Subterranean living has its advantages—your home is much cooler than the sizzling landscape of summer just outside the door and it's also warmer in the winter. The rock which makes this an ideal spot for carving out relatively safe earthen homes is a volcanic ash that blanketed the area some 640,000 years ago and piled up in layers several dozen feet in thickness. Once compacted and cemented together, the tuff (ash) became solid enough to hold shape, but still soft enough to dig into easily. Some researchers postulate that the source of this ash was a huge eruption in Yellowstone (that's right, *the* Yellowstone, some 600 miles away) which produced the Lava Creek tuff, a rock type suspiciously similar to the tuff found here.

The nice thing about living underground is it's cooler in the summer AND warmer in the winter, especially if you install a wood-burning stove like they did here. You can still see the stovepipes sticking out of the ground from the living areas way below.

Who says you can't get creative with subterranean architecture? Here the elaborate Southern Antebellum design is accented by Venetian windows and tastefully capped by a simple Italian-influenced frieze with bold hints of Renaissance revival. Bravo!

IF YOU GO . . .

contact info: Death Valley Visitor Information, phone: (760) 786-3200; www.nps.gov/deva

fee: Death Valley has a per-vehicle entrance fee that is good for 7 days

hours: open during daylight hours

lodging: several campgrounds and resorts offer the full spectrum of accommodations inside the park

aboveground: if you're going into Death Valley (and I hope you are, considering you're so close) make sure to check out the Eureka Mine; see the listing for it in this guide

10

Eagle and High Peak Mine

type of site: historic underground gold mine

skill level: 2

equipment needed: not much needed except a jacket and a camera

temperature: approximately 50 degrees

tour length: varies according to needs of the patrons; plan a couple hours if you're just dropping in

description: The Eagle and High Peak Mine is a combination of two formerly separate mines, two competing operations that were united as one after World War I. Together they extend more than 1000 feet into the mountain, utilizing eleven working levels with a vertical distance of 500 feet.

The usual tour travels along the main horizontal tunnel, showing off the mine's timbering, its feeder chutes, ore carts, and all the tools used to dig out the ore. Most tours visit two levels of the mine where your guide explains both the machinery and methodology used to transport the rock to the surface. The tour is completed at the hoist room with machinery that carried miners 500 feet down into the mine and back out again. Huge stamps just outside the mine were used to crush the ore to extract the gold on-site.

This place is a small-time operation with a down-home feel. It gives you a real glimpse into the gritty, elemental existence of hard-rock mining of the nineteenth century and you come away with a true feeling of the way it was for most underground operations of that time.

directions: This mine is just outside Julian, which is about 45 miles northeast of San Diego on Route 79. From 79 follow C Street uphill (north). In 2 blocks the road gets a little rough. At 0.2 miles from the turn, bear left (there's a sign) and then take a right onto the entrance road.

precautions: This is private property. Do not enter it unless a) the gate is open, b) you made an appointment or, c) you were invited by the management (see "a" above). If you choose to ignore all the signs, I'm not gonna come to bail you out of jail!

ABOVE: *Much of the original equipment that was used to operate the mine is still in place.*

RIGHT: *The entrance to the property is well marked but don't even think of entering it unless it's open for business.*

BELOW: *Another example of cool mining equipment for you to ogle over.*

This mine has a lot of history and is the genuine experience.

IF YOU GO . . .

contact info: Eagle and High Peak Mine, phone: (760) 765-0036
fee: per-person fee; group rates available
hours: by appointment or when the gate is open
lodging: camping in Anza Borrego Desert State Park; lodging in Julian
aboveground: Anza Borrego Desert State Park is just to the east; check out the "pie wars" in the town of Julian; everyone in town has their own opinion as to who has the best

11

Empire Mine

type of site: historic gold mine and grounds

skill level: 1

equipment needed: none—except bring a camera and plenty of memory for the camera

temperature: most of this site is aboveground and outside so whatever the weather is, you're stuck with it

tour length: you can spend as little as a couple hours or most of a day

description: This is the best single educational mining experience in the state. You'll not find a better display of hard-rock mining equipment, techniques and artifacts anywhere. The property has many of the original buildings and structures—including the offices—all of which are outfitted in authentic period accoutrements and artifacts. You can also visit the Bourn family home, which still stands on site and is a fabulous tour all by itself. (The Bourn family was one of the original owners of Empire Mine.) Park staff give regular tours of the home, the mine, and the grounds.

The only thing lacking here is an underground tour. The main shaft that was used to transport both miners and ore is front-and-center in the mine yard and you are welcome to visit it. Inside you can see the dual tracks headed down-shaft for hundreds of feet but, alas, you cannot follow them—twenty feet below the surface the shaft is blocked-off by a large gate. There are plans to open another tunnel for full-on underground adventures, but when that might happen is anyone's guess.

directions: From route 20/49 in Grass Valley—exit at Empire Street and head south for 1.4 miles to the main parking area.

precautions: It can get awfully hot in the summer, so carry sunscreen and lots of water. All bathroom facilities are outside the main entrance. So make sure to go before you go in.

geology

Sometimes a rock isn't just a rock. Consider the case of George Roberts, a local fellow whose primary interest in 1850 was trees. One day Roberts was wandering the hills near Grass Valley surveying for timber. He wasn't impressed by the prospects. Then his eyes fell upon a quartz vein. Upon closer investigation he noticed the white rock was interlaced with a yellowish material—gold! By luck Roberts had stumbled upon a classic "lode" deposit of gold where elemental native gold mixed in with the crystallized matrix rock, in this case quartz. George sold his interest in the Ophir Vein and moved on. It was one of the richest hard-rock gold deposits in the state; over 5.8 million ounces of gold were extracted here.

history

Be sure to visit the North Star Mine Powerhouse, located nearby. It is an amazing collection of power-harnessing equipment, including the largest Pelton wheel ever constructed (30 feet in diameter) which is still on its original footings. The powerhouse also includes many more geology displays and rock mining artifacts.

Although this is an original entrance that plunges thousands of feet into the hillside, you can't go very far underground in this shaft. However, as of this writing, Empire Mine is planning a new shaft that will allow visitors to tour the below-ground workings safely.

The mine yard has literally tons of equipment on display.

ABOVE: *The "mucker" goes in after a blast and scoops up the piles of "muck" produced by blowing lots of rocks to bits.*

RIGHT: *Mines use lots of pumps, like this one here. Maybe it works, probably it doesn't, but it sure looks cool rusting away in the mine yard.*

ABOVE: *The North Star Mine Powerhouse is a great addition to the Empire Mine visit and is only a couple miles away. Here is an example of the power-generating equipment that was used in the days before gasoline engines.*

RIGHT: *Some of the largest Pelton wheels ever made were used nearby.*

PELTON TYPE
WATER WHEEL
PRODUCED 71000 HP AT 327 RPM, DIAMETER 30 FT
WEIGHT 26,000 LBS, BUILT BY ALLIS CHALMERS
OF SINGLE CAST NICKEL STEEL
GIFT OF OROVILLE-WYANDOTTE IRRIGATION DIST
DEDICATED SEPTEMBER 1997
BY NEVADA COUNTY HISTORICAL SOCIETY

The primary building that housed the Empire Mine offices is nicely restored and available to explore.

IF YOU GO . . .

contact info: Empire Mine, phone: (530) 273-8522; www.empiremine.org/
fee: per-person fee; group rates available
hours: summer (May–September) 9–6; winter (October–April) 10–5; closed
   Thanksgiving, Christmas, New Year's Day
lodging: improved camping and lodging in immediate area of Grass Valley
   and Nevada City
aboveground: almost all of this site is aboveground

12

Eureka Mine

type of site: historic underground gold mine

skill level: 3

equipment needed: flashlights and/or head lamps; hard hats are a good idea whenever you go underground, but they're not absolutely necessary here so long as you go slowly and watch the ceiling

temperature: influenced by ambient temperatures

tour length: self-guided, 1 hour or more

description: It's a pleasant feeling when the temps are hitting 110 degrees at Furnace Creek (appropriate name, wouldn't you say?) and you're hanging out far above the valley, exploring the inside of a mine tunnel where it's a perfect 75 degrees. This wonderful little adventure is a self-guided underground mine with one main tunnel and a substantial branch-off, both of which run along an easy, horizontal pattern. Don't worry, you can't get lost. The original workings of the mine have been made safe by the National Park Service, which constructed steel nets over the dangerous areas so unsuspecting tourists (and kids!) won't get lost or injured. Pete Aguereberry's camp is just on the other side of the hill (you passed it along the dirt road). Most of the buildings are still standing, including the cabin he lived in. Also be sure to check out Aguereberry Point, just a few miles down this same road, for an incomparable view of Death Valley and the poor sizzling folks below.

directions: Located just off the access road to Aguereberry Point in Death Valley. From Stovepipe Wells, head west on State Route 190 about 8 miles. Turn left onto Emigrant Canyon Road (paved) and drive south approximately 17 miles to the sign for Aguereberry Point. Set your odometer to zero and turn left onto the maintained dirt road. In about 1.5 miles you'll see abandoned buildings at the base of a low hill on your right—this is where Pete Aguereberry lived. At 1.7 miles the road forks—take the right fork, which bends around hill. (The turn here is NOT marked.) Park in the turn-around about 0.2 miles from the fork. The mine entrance is just to the west, visible from the parking area.

precautions: Although the dangerous areas inside the mine itself have been sectioned off, outside the tunnels there is a lot of loose rock, decrepit buildings, and old mine workings that could pose a hazard. Be careful and do not climb on any structures.

history

If you've ever been here when the thermometer gets nasty and cranks up the sizzle way past 100, then you'll understand why they call it Death Valley. The heat can get downright volcanic. Yet sometimes God watches over fools, even here in the middle of summer. Pete Aguereberry was just such a fool and arrived here in 1905 with no clue what he was getting into. In June of that year he attempted to cross Death Valley alone and nearly lost his life in the process. Luckily he was found and nursed back to health by the caretaker of a local ranch. Unfazed, a month later Pete teamed up with Shorty Harris and they decided to head west to Ballarat to check out the prospecting there. But along the way Pete found an outcrop which looked promising and determined that it contained the real thing—gold. The digging started in earnest shortly thereafter as a more-or-less joint project between Pete and Shorty, both of whom had filed gold claims on the hill. By 1907 the mine was tied up in a litigation battle which ultimately settled with Pete gaining control of the claims. He lived and worked at the mine from 1907 until the early 1930s when his health began to fail. Except for occasional help from friends and relatives, the Eureka mine was built and worked almost exclusively by Pete, a feat which gained him some notoriety. Pete Aguereberry died on Nov. 23, 1945 and is buried in Lone Pine, California.

Pete Aguereberry lived just over the hill from the mine entrance at what became known as Aguereberry Camp.

Much of the original tracks, timbering, and hand-hewn mine workings are still in place just the way Pete Aguereberry left it.

ABOVE: The tracks heading out to the entrance, left just as they were.

RIGHT: Watch your head, especially if you forgot your hard hat. The ceilings are pretty low in much of the mine.

ABOVE: *Although abandoned over 60 years ago, some parts of the main frame still abide along this hillside.*

RIGHT: *Part of Aguereberry Camp, where Pete lived and had his workshops.*

BELOW: *Do NOT climb on these structures. They will fall down and so will you.*

An ore chute from upper levels allowed quick loading into the carts below. The structures inside are labeled so you can get an idea of how things worked here back in the day.

IF YOU GO . . .

contact info: Death Valley Visitor Information, phone: (760) 786-3200; www.nps.gov/deva

fee: Death Valley has a per-vehicle entrance fee that is good for 7 days

hours: open during daylight hours

lodging: several campgrounds and resorts offer the full spectrum of accommodations inside the park

aboveground: don't just stand there—do something! Death Valley is one of the unsung gems of the National Park Service; get out and enjoy it while you're here; make sure to check out the "caves" at Dublin Gultch near Shoshone

Gold Cliff Mine

type of site: historic underground gold mine

skill level: 3.5

equipment needed: basic equipment is provided (hard hat, head lamps, gloves, and coveralls); wear boots, rugged clothes and bring water, snacks and a camera

temperature: generally 65–75 degrees

tour length: guided *Adventure Trip* takes 2½–3½ hours

description: Folks often think the life of a '49er was one hardscrabble day after another without a break in the dismal forecast. And sure, it was no joyride—dawn-to-dark work of hard labor. But some of those old prospectors appreciated the environment and the perks their life of toil sometimes provided. Take, for instance, working in the Sierras. I don't care what you're doing, you cannot help but sometimes enjoy the majesty of the area. And this is one of those places. Located in the heart of the Mother Lode, the Gold Cliff Mine *Adventure Trip* is a truly unique experience, combining the awesome natural underworld with impressive tunnels created by miners practicing their craft.

Visitors meet their guide at the mine site, where they are issued the necessary gear and receive instructions and orientation. The expedition begins with a brief surface tour that relates historical tales about the area, discussion of the mining operations here, and the function of many structures that once stood on the property. In its heyday between 1899 and 1920, the Gold Cliff Mine's shaft descended about 1,900 feet beneath the surface. During the course of its run, Gold Cliff produced almost 3 million dollars worth of gold.

directions: Gold Cliff Mine is located near the town of Angels Camp. However, because these are reservation-only adventures, you must first sign up for a trip before receiving exact directions and maps to the site.

precautions: This is much more rigorous than a walking tour and is not for the woefully out-of-shape. It includes scrambling and hiking over loose rock and negotiating steep terrain (40–50 degree slopes) with the use of ropes.

geology

There's some serious exploration in store as the guides navigate you through the mine's deeper passages and chambers. The route includes steep diagonal hiking, climbing, and crawling using knotted hand-lines on a 45- to 50-degree slope, and negotiating loose rubble. The total distance traveled is approximately one mile and includes exploration of two large chambers, rafting across a flooded 100-foot deep mine, and the possibility of seeing bats, millipedes, and other creatures.

After returning to the surface, you'll continue on to the 200-ton stamp mill and to a second mine location. The vertical entrance is hidden within a picturesque precipice overlooking a canopy of trees. Using hand-lines to descend, groups make their way into the shaft where the actual mine entrance is revealed. This smaller mine contains a seasonal lake of clear water and beautiful examples of calcite formations including flowstone, ribbons and soda straws. Some of these appear purple, a very rare color in caves. This suggests some strange mineralogy is going on here.

There's a crystal-clear lake at the bottom and even a raft to get around in!

What happens when you remove a lot of rock from a hole in the ground? Well, for one thing, you just created an underground play land!

IF YOU GO . . .

contact info: general information, phone: 866-762-2837;
www.caverntours.com/Gold_Cliff.html

fee: per-person fee, no group rates; participant numbers are limited

hours: open every day but this adventure is by advance reservation only

lodging: incredible camping at Calaveras Big Trees State Park; lodging in Murphys and Angels Camp

aboveground: also visit Moaning Cavern and Natural Bridges nearby; both Angels Camp and Murphys are historic towns

14

Hall City Cave

type of site: active limestone cavern

skill level: 3

equipment needed: flashlights and/or head lamps; hard hats are a good idea, but not absolutely necessary here

temperature: influenced by ambient temperature

tour length: self-guided, about 1 hour

description: We included this site because it's a nice drive, a beautiful hike and a pleasant stroll through the woods. But don't expect a whole lot from the cave itself. The entrance is a typical collapsed sink with some logs/ladders leaning in it to make the scrambling in and out easier. This is followed by a short passage with a few formations, some of which are, admittedly nice, especially considering how accessible they are. But before you know it, in a hundred feet or so, the passage ends at a couple small lakes. *Do not* attempt to swim through the lakes as they go nowhere except down. This is no joke, just ask any caver in Florida about "cave-diving." They'll tell you people drown every year trying it—some of them professionals. I repeat: *Do not attempt this. It's basically suicide.*

directions: Begin at the stealthy little town of Wildwood in Trinity County. It lies in hiding about 2.6 miles north of State Route 36 on Wildwood Road, which intersects 36 about 50 miles west of Red Bluff. From Wildwood head east on Wildwood Road toward 36. Just outside the town you'll cross the bridge over Hayfork Creek. In about one tenth of a mile there's a bend in the road and a gravel road intersecting on the left. Set your odometer to 0.0 and turn left onto Forest Road 30N04. At 0.8 miles, bear right onto 29N07. This is a narrow, winding road with poor visibility, so go slow. At 3.1 miles turn left onto 29N07A at the sign that reads "Hall City Cave ½ mile." (There are no other signs for the cave beyond this point.) At 3.4 miles there will be a blocked road and a turn-around. Park at the small area next to the creek below the gate. The unmarked trail branches off the back of this lot and follows along the creek. Follow this trail upstream about ¼ mile until it crosses the creek. About 75 yards past the crossing, another major trail comes into this one from the left at a large Douglas fir tree. Take this trail uphill through a couple switchbacks to the cave entrance.

precautions: There are several mines in this area with unsecured entrances. These are *very dangerous* places. DO NOT enter any of them.

history

You gotta love legends! If it wasn't for them we'd have little to talk about, especially in regards to this cave. One fairly plausible story tells of local Indians using the cave as a burial vault, much as they did in other caverns (Moaning Cavern, California Caverns and so on). But that's pretty boring stuff when compared to my favorite, which revolves around two local fellows that were beset by Indians who pursued them up into the hills. As it happens, on the day in question these fellows had some undisclosed amount of—pick one: gold, silver, diamonds, or cash. Being the Good Old Boys they were, our protagonists became somewhat worried about their pension plans and decided the best thing to do was to drop the bags into the lake at the back of the nearby cave, thereby lightening their load and helping them escape from their pursuers. At this point things get a little fuzzy. Depending upon your references, the two were: a) killed by the Indians who just plain didn't like Good Old Boys and couldn't care less about what was in the sacks or, b) escaped the scene and returned later only to find out the lakes were bottomless and thus swallowed up their stash or c) escaped but never made it back to the cave because they couldn't find it and eventually went mad searching the hills for their lost treasure.

It's not big—in fact it's pretty small!—but there are a few nice formations.

It's far off the beaten trail, but the drive is pleasant, the hike peaceful, and the scenery wonderful. So what if the cave is minimal? It's just part of the journey, not the destination.

ABOVE: *The advantage of such a short caving trip is you can't get lost in here.*

RIGHT: *View from just inside the sinkhole entrance.*

ABOVE: *The entrance drops down into a small sinkhole but someone built a ladder to help us out here.*

RIGHT: *The best formations are in the back.*

BELOW: *Moss covers the rocks flanking the entrance.*

WARNING: There are several old mine workings in the area that have not been sealed shut. Do NOT enter any of them—they are unstable and very dangerous. This is one such site.

IF YOU GO . . .

contact info: Hayfork Ranger Station, phone: 530-628-5227
fee: no fee
hours: daylight hours
lodging: camping on Shasta-Trinity National Forest land; closest lodging is in Hayfork
aboveground: this is one of the most scenic areas in California, as it's close to the shore and to wine country; hey, why not do both? Go for a tour, grab a bottle of wine, and then watch the sunset at Trinidad

15

Hole-in-the-Wall

type of site: natural cavities in lava flow

skill level: 3–4

equipment needed: good boots and rugged clothing—the rocks here are gritty, sharp, and unforgiving; carry plenty of water

temperature: this area can become an oven in the summer; if it's a sunny day, the rock can heat up 30 degrees more than the ambient air temperature

tour length: self-guided—1 hour at least; plan to spend a few hours if not all day

description: There's a lot more to Hole-in-the-Wall than just a hole-in-the-wall. In fact there are a lot of holes in a lot of walls around here and lots more that aren't in any walls at all. Stop in at the visitor center for a good overview of the place and a map of the local trails. Just about any trail from the parking area will give you a good feeling for this weird volcanic geology. The most popular trail is, of course, the short one to the nearby overlook. It's just on the south side of the parking area. For a more in-your-face, rugged adventure try the "Rings Trail", a half-mile loop that comes off the center of the parking lot. According to an 1800s legend, Indians escaped local up-in-arms ranchers by descending down Banshee Canyon and disappearing from view in the myriad cracks, crags, nooks and cavities. Now you can follow their footsteps with the help of metal rings mounted in the rock. But hopefully you don't need to elude a posse of wild cowboys and can take things a little more carefully as a result. This is also a great place to visit on the way to Mitchell Caverns, which is located only a few minutes away.

directions: This is part of Mojave National Preserve. From I-40 exit #100 follow Essex Road north 10 miles to the junction with Black Canyon Road and turn right. Hole-in-the-Wall is 10 miles north on Black Canyon Road. Watch for the signs to the visitor center.

precautions: Avoid midsummer heat. And be careful as you explore this labyrinthine maze—the rockscape is, if anything, completely unpredictable. Follow the trails, and go slowly and cautiously.

Hole-in-the-Wall

geology

The strange, wild patterns of cavities, tunnels and tubes found at Hole-in-the-Wall are a result of super gaseous volcanic flatulence combined with sticky, gooey, magmatic ooze. Does that sound gross or what?! OK, so it's not exactly a scientific definition, but in most volcanic eruptions the greatest volume of material occurs in gaseous form. There was a large volume of gases here under pressure mixed with rhyolite (a volcanic rock rich in silica). As this mixture escaped, the gases expanded, creating bubbles. Some of these bubbles reached the lava surface and popped; others remained trapped. Soon after, the lava cooled and preserved the weird patterns now evident at Hole-in-the-Wall.

history

It's a good thing you weren't living here 18 million years ago. Life was getting pretty testy about then. There was a colossal argument going on between magma and the surface rock trying to hold it down. Eventually, the whole situation ended in a series of violent eruptions. Huge blocks of rock—some 60 feet in diameter!—were blasted skyward. Spewing ash rained down over the landscape, while viscous, rhyolitic lava oozed out of the earth. Things finally quieted down after a million years, but all-in-all it was not a pretty sight. The local cops declined comment, saying it was a "domestic dispute."

Just a few of the "holes" for which this area is named.

Look! A wall with a hole in it! There are so many walls with holes you'd be hard pressed to figure out which one is the namesake. Luckily, the visitor center is very near the Hole-in-the-Wall and the rangers can point you to it.

ABOVE: *The Rings Climb is a trip on the wild side. It's fun, but you don't want to try it if you're woefully out of shape.*

RIGHT: *If you go past the overlooks near the parking areas, be ready for some real rough-and-tumble rock work. The good news is that no one is forcing you to.*

ABOVE: *The rock formations here are wild, weird, and unusual. To really get a feel for it all, stop off at the visitor center/museum. It's right here at Hole-in-the-Wall.*

RIGHT: *Now which rock did I leave my car keys on . . .*

There's a whole lot of holes in this ancient lava flow. Now get out there and find them!

IF YOU GO . . .

contact info: Mojave Visitor Information, phone: 760-252-6100;
www.nps.gov/moja/index.htm

fee: no fee, but make a donation at the Hole-in-the-Wall Visitor Center to
help out with the upkeep

hours: open every day except that the visitor center has limited hours

lodging: basic camping in the preserve; closest lodging is in Needles or Barstow

aboveground: visitor center/museum; guided nature hikes all around,
plus you're in The Mojave National Preserve, enjoy it! For a deeper
underground experience, Mitchell Caverns is nearby

16

Jot Dean Ice Cave

type of site: a lava tube with an active seasonal ice trap

skill level: 3.5

equipment needed: good boots and warm, rugged clothing are necessary; you could get by with just a flashlight, but basic caving equipment is strongly advisable—hard hat with a head lamp, flashlights, knee pads, coveralls, and gloves

temperature: summer, 32–40 degrees; winter, below 32

tour length: self-guided–1 hour or more

description: There's nothing quite like walking into a natural ice cave in the middle of a hot day. This is one of our favorites, primarily because of the ultra-cool layered ice wall that has formed in the hollows of the tube. It's incredibly photogenic—clear, layered, massive ice piled more than six feet high. The cave has been collecting ice since the last glaciers retreated, about 8,000 years ago. It always has ice, although in recent years the amount that hangs around for the summer has been diminishing, thanks primarily to global warming.

directions: From Bartle (which is about 30 miles east of Mt. Shasta City on 89), follow State Route 89 about half a mile east to the intersection with Forest Route 15 (Harris Springs Road). Set your odometer to 0.0 here and turn north on 15. At 4.3 miles the road forks and Route 15 branches off to the left. Head right following Forest Route 49. At 7.0 miles Route 3 branches to the right, but you stay left on 49. At about 17.2 miles you'll see lava flows. At 21.9 miles turn left into the parking area for Jot Dean Ice Cave. There is a sign. The cave entrance is less than 100 yards from the parking area. The main part is entered by negotiating down the western side of the collapse, along a short trail. You then duck into an overhang and will instantly feel the temperature drop.

precautions: This is an unimproved natural lava tube. The rock is sharp and footing is unstable. Be especially careful entering the cave—ice occurs very near the entrance. On one trip I unexpectedly encountered a sloping ice sheet, fell squarely on my butt and rode uncontrollably to the bottom where I hit the spiny lava wall. Luckily the ride was short and I had my helmet on. As a result, we'd recommend you get on your butt as soon as you get into the cave and take it very slowly.

geology

Here's a good trick question to impress friends at your local geology club trivia party: What's the largest volcano in California? They, of course, will be smitten with their endless depth of geotrivia, altogether certain of the answer. But if they cite Mt. Lassen or Mt. Shasta, which they likely will, you can politely inform them they've totally blown it. The largest volcano in the state doesn't even look like a volcano. The Medicine Lake Volcano covers an area 15 miles wide by 25 miles long and is actually far larger in mass than either of the two giants listed above. The Medicine Lake Volcano is a shield volcano, a type of volcano with gently sloping sides. In this respect, it looks much different than the more well-known stratovolcanoes—tall, cone-shaped volcanoes like Washington State's Mount St. Helens. The Medicine Lake Volcano had its rock-and-roll heyday about 100,000 years ago and has been grooving to the mellower tunes of B.B. King ever since.

It's fairly easy to get into but you must be VERY CAREFUL once inside—the floors are uneven and the rocks are covered with ice. Be sure to have flashlights and go SLOWLY.

It's 98 degrees outside but you'll be cool as a cucumber in this natural ice box.

IF YOU GO . . .

contact info: Shasta-Trinity National Forest McCloud Ranger Station, phone: 530-964-2184

fee: no fee

hours: daylight hours

lodging: camping on Shasta-Trinity National Forest land; closest lodging is Mt. Shasta

aboveground: you're right next to Lava Beds National Monument, and just about within sight of Mt. Shasta; what more do you want?

17

Lake Shasta Caverns

type of site: active horizontal limestone cave complex

skill level: 2

equipment needed: nothing other than common sense and a camera.

temperature: 68 degrees year-round

tour length: the total round-trip time from the visitor center runs about 2 hours

description: If you had to choose a setting for a great limestone cavern, you'd be hard pressed to find a place more spectacular than that of Lake Shasta Caverns, situated high on a hill, overlooking the blue and beautiful Shasta Lake. In this context, Lake Shasta Caverns is one of the more unusual caving adventures you will ever experience and unless you're a member of the NSS (National Speleological Society) assigned to actively investigate karst regions around lakes and reservoirs, you are not likely to experience this kind of adventure in your lifetime. It all begins with a boat ride across the emerald green lake narrated by your captain. Then there's a scenic and informative bus trip up the escarpment to the entrance. By the time you get to the cave itself, you feel as though you could ace the geology classes at the local community college. But then the fun really begins. The cavern is filled with every kind of cave formation, in a rainbow of colors. The fairly easy tour follows a roughly horizontal cave pattern but it does include some series of rises, the longest of which is about 80 steps. There are nine "rooms" serving up the standard speleological fare of stalactites, stalagmites and soda straws in profusion. As such, you're guaranteed not to go away hungry at this spelunking table. In addition there are some great helictites (strange, gravity defying rarities in the world down under) and wonderful draperies. Eventually you exit from the cave on a cliff face—protected by railings—with a breathtaking view of the Shasta Lake and the surrounding landscape.

directions: From Redding, follow I-5 approximately 17 miles north to exit #695. Turn east onto Shasta Caverns Road and follow signs. Parking area is about 1.5 miles from I-5.

precautions: As you exit the cave there is a ridge trail back to the bus which is somewhat exposed to heights. Keep kids under control.

history

It sounds like something out of the Beverly Hillbillies: While out hunting one day in 1878, a local fellow named J.A. Richardson was pursuing some game up the steep embankment when he happened upon the hidden entrance to a cave. Over the next year or so, he made several trips inside but apparently didn't tell many folks about it, probably because its entrance was so hard to get to, and, well, there wasn't any gold anyway, so who cares . . .

Some decades later, when the concept of visiting caves was becoming popular to the folks of nearby Redding, a group of interlopers attempted to take credit for the discovery. They even went so far as to scratch out Richardson's words wherever they found them, inserting their own signatures and their bogus "date of discovery." But J.A. was no fool—he posted his name several places in the underground chambers and told not a soul about the locations. As a result, some of his lines were never discovered by the false prophets. Years later, however, they were found by modern expeditions, thus ensuring Richardson's rightful credit to the pioneering discovery.

Richardson was no fool—the proof is in the penmanship.

Too bad they don't have a restaurant here—you sure can't beat the view of Lake Shasta.

ABOVE: *There's a wealth of speleothems inside.*
RIGHT: *Stalactites crowd the ceilings and walls.*

ABOVE: *Curtains along the pathway.*

RIGHT: *In prior years they used makeshift ladders to access some of the more difficult parts.*

BELOW: *There's a lot to see in the hills above Lake Shasta.*

Lake Shasta Caverns is one of the nicest caves in California. Here's just a glimpse of why it is.

IF YOU GO . . .

contact info: Lake Shasta Caverns, phone: 1-800-795-CAVE;
www.lakeshastacaverns.com

fee: per-person fee includes boat, bus, and cave tour; group discounts

hours: open daily except during very severe weather; closed Thanksgiving
and Christmas

lodging: camping available around the lake; lodging in Redding

aboveground: gift shop, historical museum, gold panning, gemstone mining,
picnic area, all on site; the area around Shasta Lake is full of hiking and
water sports; this is the place to hang out on hot summer days

18

Lava Beds National Monument

type of site: multiple lava tubes of various sizes, complexity, and length

skill level: from 2–5, depending on the lava tube

equipment needed: in many of the shorter tubes with improved access you could get by with just a flashlight, but as a matter of safety, we recommend always using basic caving equipment, especially in longer or more complex tubes; bring a hard hat with a head lamp, flashlight, knee pads, coveralls, and gloves

temperature: influenced by ambient temperatures

tour length: self-guided—you can spend as little as a few hours here or a whole summer; some cave tours are also led by the park rangers

description: If you're into lava tubes, then this is your nirvana. Lava Beds National Monument has so many lava tubes you'd think that some space aliens went berserk plowing holes all over the place looking for tasty Earthling victims to gobble up. At last count there were over 700 different lava tubes of varying shapes, sizes and complexity within the park. This porous landscape is so riddled with holes you could spend a whole summer exploring here and barely scratch the subsurface. Much of this geologic diversity has occurred fairly recently—over the last half-million years or so. Several stages of volcanic eruptions on the Medicine Lake shield volcano are responsible for creating the intriguing, rugged landscape here.

directions: From Dorris, take U.S. 97 about 3 miles north to California Highway 161 (known as Stateline Road) and turn right. Travel east on CA 161 through the Lower Klamath National Wildlife Refuge about 17 miles to Hill Road. Turn right (south) following the signs. In about 12 miles or so you'll enter Lava Beds National Monument and intersect with the main road throughout the park near Gillem's Camp. The visitor center is about 9 miles south of this point.

precautions: Many of the lava tubes are easily accessed and well mapped with no real surprises. Regardless of which ones you enter, take it slow. Some tubes have multiple levels, others have branch-offs, and some have unstable roofs. Many of the more remote ones are seldom visited and have a higher element of danger. Be sure to tell someone where you're going and when you'll be back. Always carry plenty of water.

geology

The Medicine Lake volcano has been a pretty rowdy place in the last half million years or so—spawning all manner of geologic offspring. Chief among the delights are the famous lava tubes. These natural tunnels form when a lava "river" exits from a subsurface channel in a lava flow leaving a roofed tunnel in its place (imagine soda exiting a straw). When conditions are right in volcanic areas, lava tubes can be very abundant.

history

Culturally, this area is considered one of the longest continually-occupied areas in North America, with history and cultural legacy stretching back thousands of years. Then there are historical events like the Modoc War. During the winter of 1872-1873, a small band of Modoc Indians used an intimate knowledge of their homeland's terrain to their tactical advantage. Under the leadership of Kintpuash (nicknamed "Captain Jack" by non-natives), the Modocs took refuge in "Captain Jack's Stronghold," a rugged, natural lava "fortress." From here the Modocs held off US Army forces—numbering up to ten times their strength—for over five months before being defeated at the Battle of Dry Lake. This defeat led to the capture of Captain Jack and the end of the war.

Catacombs Cave is a fun lava tube experience with some branches you must crawl through. But be careful here; this is one lava tube confusing enough to get lost in. Keep the kids on a leash.

Lava tubes are notorious for being difficult to negotiate. But here the National Park Service has done their best to make many of the finer examples easily accessible to you.

ABOVE: *Groovin' inside the tube at Golden Dome.*
RIGHT: *Garden Bridges Cave.*

ABOVE: *There are several places in the park which host rock art. The most famous is petroglyph point where one entire side is home to thousands of pecked images.*

RIGHT: *An example of the pictographs that you can see here.*

BELOW: *A view from the underground.*

It's rugged land, to be sure. But it's one of rugged beauty, all the same.

IF YOU GO . . .

contact info: Lava Beds N.M., phone: 530-667-8100;
www.nps.gov/labe/index.htm

fee: per-vehicle entrance fee to the park

hours: park is always open; visitor center is open daily except Christmas
Eve and Christmas Day

lodging: basic camping in the Monument; closest lodging is in Klamath
Falls, Oregon

aboveground: the visitor center/museum is great, so check it out; there are
many other interesting aspects to this park and tons of hiking; they also
offer guided walks with the rangers

19

Maggie Mine

type of site: historic underground silver mine

skill level: 1

equipment needed: it's got lights, props and kitschy mannequins, so all you need is a little curiosity and a camera

temperature: influenced by ambient temperatures in a good way, it's generally cooler than outside in the summer, warmer in the winter

tour length: self-guided—an hour or less; there's one main tunnel with a branch-off; the total length is about 1000 feet

description: The folks at Knott's Berry Farm have done you a good turn by restoring this town and one of its mines. The Maggie Mine comes complete with periodic alcoves showing off vignettes of prospectors doing their hard-rock mining thing in the nineteenth century underground. There's also real mining equipment and period furnishings. All in all, it's informative and fun, especially for kids.

You'll notice the underground workings here have little in the way of "timbering," the support framework used to shore up the roof of mines and prevent them from collapsing. The nice thing about the "Maggie" is that most of the hard rock which they blasted through was very solid and thus supported itself admirably, precluding the need in most parts for extra support. This, undoubtedly, was a great plus for the mine owners, as a substantial portion of the cost of mining is the timbering. Another nice aspect for you is you won't conk your head on the roof!

directions: Located in the restored Calico Ghost Town. From Barstow follow I-15 northeast about 7 miles to exit #191 at Ghost Town Road. Drive north about 3 miles to the entrance.

precautions: Watch out for them rowdy gunslingers—they're apt to appear on the town streets any old time. Don't get caught in the cross-fire!

history

There's a lot of mystery in ghost towns like Calico. All we know about the Maggie Mine is that a widow with the last name of Mulcahy moved to Calico in 1884. What happened to her husband, how it happened, and why it happened, is anybody's guess. The widow Mulcahy had 5 boys and they all took to mining. The price of silver was strong at the time and Calico was squarely on the mining boom map. With 5 strong boys working 14-hour days, a family could rake in a few bucks. Things were looking up for Calico in those days—there were over a thousand people in residence working 50 mines and the town boasted 22 saloons. There was also a thriving red-light district. But by 1896 the price of silver had dropped, most of the easy veins had been played out, and much of the town was abandoned. Still, three of the brothers remained. By 1916 John Mulcahy had bought the workings and named it the Maggie Mine. Who Maggie was and how exactly she got a mine named after her is anyone's guess. Some speculate he named it "Maggie" in keeping with a song that was popular at the time. Personally I think he listened to too much Rod Stewart, but I might be wrong about that detail. Despite the fatal drop in silver value, John kept up the mine and used it as a convenient underground home.

Calico is unlike any other ghost town you'll see. It's been completely reborn thanks to the generosity of Walter Knott (of Knott's Berry Farm fame) who helped restore the town and then donated it to the county.

Despite being built over 100 years ago, many of the original structures of Calico still abide here.

IF YOU GO . . .

contact info: Calico Ghost Town general information, phone:
   1-800-TO-CALICO; www.calicotown.com/index.php
fee: per-person fee to enter town; another small fee to tour the mine
hours: open every day except Christmas
lodging: improved camping on site; lodging in Barstow
aboveground: well don't blame me if you can't find anything to do in Calico;
   I mean, come on! There's an entire reconstructed ghost town
   to explore; you can even shop here!

20

Mercer Caverns

type of site: active vertical and horizontal limestone cavern

skill level: 2

equipment needed: none necessary, although you may want to bring a jacket since it is fairly cool inside

temperature: constant 55°F

tour length: guided tours are about 45 minutes long

description: Enter on the scene a 31-year-old prospector by the name of Walter J. Mercer. On a hot summer day in 1885, Mr. Mercer was returning home from a frustrating round of prospecting. *Seems like everyone's finding gold except me*, he mused. Hot, tired, and thirsty, Walt noticed a limestone outcrop and thinking he might find water there, went over to take a look. Nope, no water. He slumped to the ground. *Darn, just my luck*, he thought. While thus reclined, Walt's attention was drawn to the movement of some dry grass. There wasn't any wind but somehow this grass was dancing around. Upon closer inspection he found a small opening in the Earth exhausting a strong draft of cool air. He picked up a rock and dropped it into the hole. It fell a l-o-n-g ways down. Now Walt was curious. He went to a mining camp and brought back enough tools to enlarge the opening and squeeze inside. And that was that. *To heck with all this prospecting hogwash*, he thought, *I'm gonna open me a tourist cave!*

directions: Pay attention here because you could easily miss the turn: From downtown Murphys follow Main Street heading west. Before you reach the edge of town, on the left side of the street is a sign for Mercer Caverns pointing right, toward what looks like an alley. Turn right onto this narrow, one-way path (Sheep Ranch Road) and head up the hill. In a block it broadens and becomes a two-way. Continue on Sheep Ranch for 1.3 miles to the Mercer Cavern entrance sign where you'll turn left.

precautions: There are some low points, a few squeezes, and many steps (232 on the way back up) on this tour. But it's pretty easy even so.

geology

Cave curtains are all over the place at Mercer Caverns, and they are big! In fact some of the ones found here are among the largest you are likely to see anywhere. Cave curtains occur when solutions travel along a crack or lineation (line) which deposits a continuous row of calcite crystals that build up over time. The formation extends downward in a sheet as generations of calcite grow along the margin. The result is an elegant formation that really does look a lot like a curtain, just one that's made out of stone.

history

Eons ago, the area of Mercer Caverns was frequented by early Indian tribes who seasonally hunted the nearby hills. But when you're a tribe on the go, the question sometimes arises: what do you do when one of your group expires? Well, if you happen to have access to a nearby large cave in the earth then you may as well take advantage of it. Mercer Caverns was just the place. It's thought the cave was originally used as such by a prehistoric Indian tribe called the Yokuts. Evidence shows that the Yokuts brought at least 6 bodies to the cave opening and let them roll down inside. They found their way to the bottom of the first main chamber and settled in for a nap of a few thousand years or so.

The "cave bacon" found here really does look like the stuff you buy at the grocery store.

No shortage of cool things here! Some of the largest single cave curtains you'll ever see.

ABOVE: *The stalactites are all over the place and the walls are covered with flowing columns of all colors.*

RIGHT: *Some stages of the tour get you up-close-and-personal with the cavern environment. But don't touch! It's harmful to the formations and against the law.*

ABOVE: *The nice thing about this place is the great variety of formations all in a nice single package.*

RIGHT/BELOW: *This is part of what you'll see on the tour.*

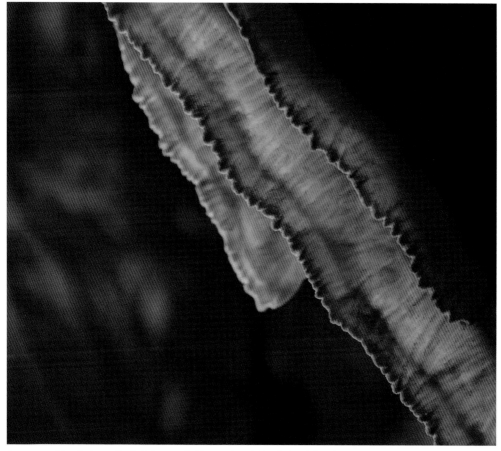

In a cave, it's all about the lighting, and this one has it in all the right places.

IF YOU GO . . .

contact info: Mercer Caverns, phone: (209) 728-2101; mercercaverns.com
fee: per-person fee; group rates available
hours: open every day; hours vary seasonally
lodging: incredible camping at Calaveras Big Trees State Park; lodging in
  Murphys and Angels Camp
aboveground: visitor center/museum, gift shop, gemstone mining, nature
  trail, picnic area; also visit Moaning Cavern and Natural Bridges

Mitchell Caverns

type of site: seasonally active horizontal limestone cavern

skill level: 1.5

equipment needed: bring your camera and curiosity; on hot days you may bring water on the hike to the cave, but all water bottles must be left outside during the tour

temperature: constant 65°F

tour length: guided tours are about 1½ hours in duration; total length is about 1½ miles in a mostly horizontal pattern

description: Jack Mitchell was nobody's fool. He knew a good thing when he saw it and when he saw this cavern, it enthralled him. Despite its remote location and a raging economic Depression, Jack opened the cave for tours in 1932. He lived in the building that is now the visitor center. Because it was so isolated (still is!), Jack built tourist cabins on site and offered his guests the option of meals as well. As entrepreneurial as he was, Jack was a regular Mr. Nice Guy, helping his friends, relatives and guests whenever the need arose. Unfortunately, in one such instance, he was working on a guest's car when it suddenly came down and crushed him. Tours abruptly halted and the state bought the property in 1954. Originally there were two separate caves along the same stratigraphic level. After the state took possession of the property, they connected the two with a tunnel. But you can't just connect two separate caverns willy-nilly. Each has its own sensitive climate with particular air pressure, currents, humidity, temperature, etc. So they installed an air-lock in the middle of the tunnel to keep them isolated.

directions: From I-40 exit #100, follow Essex Road north 10 miles to the junction with Black Canyon Road. Mitchell Caverns is 6 miles northwest of this junction on Essex Road.

precautions: Be careful along the trail to the entrance. Although well protected with railings, etc., you should keep children in hand as there are some exposed sections along this route. Also, there are some snug areas in the middle of the cavern where you must turn sideways to get through to the next room. If you have a problem with claustrophobia you may want to watch the video at the visitor center before deciding if this is for you.

history

What is it about obsessed directors and their wild movie ideas? Can't they ever let the story tell itself without getting too carried away? Apparently not. Take Oliver Stone and his epic *The Doors*, a story about Jim Morrison and his band. In one scene the screenplay called for Morrison to have a drug-induced "vision" where he wanders into a pictograph-lined cave. The place they chose for this flimsy filmy foolishness was Mitchell Caverns. And, as you can imagine, the state got carried away by the idea—not to mention the money—and allowed Oliver Stone to paint the walls of one chamber with made-up pictographs. The result was a speleological disaster which will be thousands of years in recovery. Thankfully, the best part of Mitchell Caverns remains untouched by tinsel town and you can enjoy it in all its glory.

It's in the middle of the Mojave Preserve but its not hard to get to.

Some of the plentiful formations.

ABOVE: *It's way up on a hill, but you walk along a fairly level grade from the parking lot to the cave entrance.*

RIGHT: *Some sections are a fairly intimate squeeze.*

ABOVE: *There are a few stairs along the route, but nothing to get bent about. The scenery outside is pretty cool too.*

BELOW: *The visitor center is Jack's old house and was the epicenter of the cavern community.*

RIGHT: *The scenery outside is pretty cool too.*

The tours are led by park rangers who really know their stuff, and then some!

IF YOU GO . . .

contact info: Mitchell Caverns, phone: (760) 928-2586;
www.desertusa.com/mnp/mnp_mc.html
fee: per-person fee; group rates available
hours: in summer there's 1 tour per day; in the winter there are multiple
weekend tours and 1 per day during the week
lodging: basic camping in Mojave National Preserve; lodging in Needles
aboveground: there are trails in the Providence Mountains S.R.A; stop in at
the visitor center for lists of the flora and fauna too; also visit the Mojave
National Preserve, especially Hole-in-the-Wall (see pg. 77)

Moaning Cavern

type of site: active vertical limestone cavern

skill level: 2–4

equipment needed: on the *Walking Tour* you need nothing special; if you go for the *Rappel* or the *Adventure Trip* you'll be provided the necessary equipment and instruction

temperature: constant 61 degrees year round

tour length: the *Walking Tour* and *Rappel* are both about 45 minutes long; if you're on foot, there are 234 steps on the walk down; the *Adventure Trip* is 2½–3 hours.

description: Descending down 234 stairs of a giant spiral staircase is an experience in itself. You end up 165 feet below the ground and the tour ends on the spot where scientific excavations revealed the bones of prehistoric people who had fallen into the cavern thousands of years ago. In a juxtaposition of past and present worlds, it's also the landing spot for those who choose to do the *Rappel*. Once you're at the bottom of the stairs, guides explain the history and geology of the cavern, and discuss the explorations that have traced the cavern to its current depth of 410 feet.

directions: From Angels Camp, follow Route 4 east towards Murphys. Just after Vallecito, turn right onto Parrots Ferry Road (or, from Murphys head south 3.1 miles and turn left). In another 1.3 miles turn right at sign onto Moaning Cavern Road. The parking and entrance are one mile.

precautions: This is a commercial cavern with improved walkways, steps and railings. The management advises not to carry small children in backpacks. Front packs are OK so long as you are careful in the area of low ceilings. On the *Rappel* and also the *Adventure Trip* you must be physically fit and willing to endure the standard caving situations such as getting muddy, crawling through tight spots and negotiating rough, slippery terrain.

geology

Let's say the French got mad at us for some reason and said they were gonna take back the Statue of Liberty. Where would you hide her? Well, it just so happens that there's a perfect place in the Sierras—Moaning Cavern's the place; it could hold the entire Statue of Liberty! And that's the main thrill of Moaning Cavern. Here you can rappel down 165 feet without having the slightest idea of how to do it ahead of time. And it's one of the few places in the country that allow it. Once outfitted, your equipment protects you. All you need to do is feed rope while checking out the formations as you go. There's nothing quite like sliding down this vertical playground!

history

In the visitor center you'll find a display case with the fossilized bones of Native Americans discovered in the depths of the cavern. If you look closely you'll see one particularly compelling discovery—the skull of a young native girl partially encased in calcite, evidence of its antiquity. Indians often used caves as shelters, storehouses, and ceremonial chambers. Some caves are still used as such. Combine that with the preservation capacity of such an enclosed environment and you have a natural time capsule. In fact, fossils, including human bones, are found in caves around the world.

Waves of cave curtains hanging off the wall in the lower part of the main chamber.

There's two ways down: First is the traditional hike down the largest spiral staircase you've ever seen.

ABOVE: *The Adventure Trip takes you down under where you get up close to some incredible formations. Hey, where is this guy's hard hat and gloves?*

RIGHT: *Or you can just take one small step off the top and . . . Wow!*

ABOVE: Back in the early days, things weren't as sophisticated as they are today.

BELOW: The entrance was originally just a hole in the ground.

RIGHT: People first accessed the cave via a bucket and rope. Aren't you glad you don't have to do it this way!

The formations are still active here. There are dripping ribbons and stalactites in the upper part of the main chamber.

IF YOU GO . . .

contact info: Moaning Cavern, phone: 866-762-2837;
http://www.caverntours.com/MoCavRt.htm

fee: per-person fee; group rates available; *Adventure Trip* must be reserved in advance

hours: tours daily; times vary with season

lodging: incredible camping at Calaveras Big Trees State Park; lodging in Murphys and Angels Camp

aboveground: zip-line, gemstone mining, gold panning, geode cracking, nature trail, picnic area with tables and visitor center/gift shop

23

Natural Bridges

type of site: natural travertine "bridges" formed by a creek passing through the strata

skill level: 3.5

equipment needed: in summer, when the creek is flowing, either float through on an inflatable water toy or walk/swim through if the water level is low enough; either way you should bring a change of clothes; also bring a waterproof flashlight and wear water shoes; in the winter and early spring you'll need a wet suit as the water is mighty cold then!

temperature: influenced by ambient temperatures

tour length: plan to spend at least half a day—this place is incredible

description: There are, in fact, two "bridges" here, making this probably the only place in the country which can claim such a landmark. The upper one is the most accessible and the most spectacular. It is reached via an easy ¾-mile trail from the parking area. The second is about half a mile downstream from the exit of the first and is also interesting, but not nearly as impressive as its upstream sister.

The thing to do here is to wade/swim along the creek which courses through the two underground cave systems with large natural openings at each end. The distance, in either case, is not very long but there can be some deep spots in the creek—over 8 feet—so you either have to swim or float to get all the way through. As you travel through the chambers there are some great formations and some wonderful rooms full of stalactites, flowstone, curtains and soda straws. Some of the speleothems are still active, so please do not climb on the walls or touch the formations, even in the entrance areas.

directions: From Angels Camp follow Route 4 east towards Murphys. Just after Vallecito turn right onto Parrots Ferry Road. Set your odometer to 0.0. In 1.3 miles you'll see the turn for Moaning Cavern, but continue straight on Parrots Ferry Road. At 3.7 miles you'll see a sign; the parking area for Natural Bridges is to your right.

precautions: Do not leave your car here at dark—break-ins have happened in this lot. Beware of poison oak along the trails and around the creek bed. Do not attempt this expedition during times of heavy rains. Besides the intense water flow, there is a deadly flash-flood potential. Do not take this warning lightly.

geology

The geology here is not only exciting, it is also fairly self-evident if you stop to think about it. If you could strip away the loose sediment on the surface you'd see this is a karst region. Such places are comprised of soft rock, usually limestone or marble, which erodes easily and dissolves in mild acids. In a karst area the landscape is riddled like Swiss cheese with ravines, sinkholes, cavities, and caves. At Natural Bridges, heavy deposits of travertine (accumulated layers of calcium carbonate) built up around springs that flowed adjacent to a creek. Over time this travertine piled up enough material to create a bridge over the creek, creating the massive deposits we see today. At some point the springs slowed and the growth of the deposits was arrested. The creek kept flowing and hollowed out the caverns which are now being lined with fantastic cave formations.

The caves at the lower bridge house some formations but they are not as dramatic as the upper one.

You should plan on getting wet if you really want to enjoy this adventure.

ABOVE: The shelf and exit to the lower bridge. This is the more remote of the two caves.

RIGHT: The infamous Coyote Creek, still carving marble and still looking for shortcuts.

ABOVE: *By the exit to the upper bridge.*

RIGHT/BELOW: *Spring is the best time to catch the most beauty in this setting. But, be warned, the water is cold then.*

The exit of the upper bridge is a low, broad overhang.

IF YOU GO . . .

contact info: Bureau of Reclamation New Melones Recreation & Resources Branch, phone: 209-536-9094; www.usbr.gov/mp/ccao/field_offices/new_melones/visitor_center.htm

fee: no fee

hours: daylight hours

lodging: incredible camping at Calaveras Big Trees State Park; lodging in Murphys and Angels Camp

aboveground: being as this site is so close to Moaning Cavern, you might consider making this a fantastic full-day adventure; there's a pit toilet at the parking area; there are trails along the creek and a few picnic tables

24

Packsaddle Cave

type of site: seasonally active, horizontal marble cavern

skill level: 3.5

equipment needed: flashlights and/or head lamps are a must; hard hats are a good idea whenever you go underground, but they're not absolutely necessary here so long as you go slowly and watch your footing and look out for the ceiling; take basic hiking provisions (water, food, a first aid kit) along too

temperature: high 50s–low 60s

tour length: figure a minimum of 6 hours; the hike to the cave is a 4.8-mile round-trip and gains 1315 feet in elevation, so you'll likely spend at least 3–4 hours hiking plus a couple hours in the cave

description: If you're looking for the Carlsbad Caverns of the Sierras, this cave is definitely NOT it. But if you want a nice workout in the way of a pleasant hike along the beautiful Kern River Valley, with a safe caving experience thrown in to boot, then we've got you covered here. Packsaddle cave is a mostly dry cavern that in its heyday was something spectacular. Mere relics of its glory days are still to be found in the numerous columns and flowstones that yet abide in her depths. The nice thing about this cave is it's fairly safe as "wild" caves go. It consists primarily of one big chamber right inside the entrance, with a couple dead-end offshoots to either side.

directions: From Kernville travel north on Sierra Way approximately 16 miles to Fairview Campground. Packsaddle Cave is about 2.5 miles (one-way) from the lot. After crossing the highway from the parking lot, climb 200 yards up a jeep road, then branch right onto Packsaddle Trail. A moderate to steep trail heads up over the ridge, and down into the canyon of Packsaddle Creek. The trail crosses the creek three times as it heads upstream. In the creek bed, path-finding is sometimes difficult. After the 3rd crossing, you'll follow an ephemeral tributary which angles off uphill to the left. About ¼ mile up this tributary you'll come to a signpost and a trail connecting from the hillside on your left. Follow this about ¼ mile to the large cave opening.

precautions: The hike gets steep in places and there are some stream crossings. There's also a little scrambling up the hill by the creek. Please practice good cave ethics—tread softly and don't disturb the formations.

ABOVE/RIGHT: *There's been a lot of damage here after decades of abuse by jerks who don't respect caves, but Packsaddle still has vestiges of it's former glory. Please respect all caves you enter and do not disturb the formations.*

BELOW: *The setting outside isn't bad either.*

View looking out the entrance. If you hiked up here in the middle of summer you'll be glad you're on the inside looking out.

IF YOU GO . . .

contact info: Kern River Ranger District, phone: 760-376-3781
fee: no fee unless you stay at Fairview Campground
hours: daylight hours
lodging: camping at Fairview Campground; lodging near Lake Isabella
aboveground: there are lots of great activities at the campground, including swimming, kayaking, and hiking

25

Pinnacles National Monument

type of site: talus caves—natural structural caves along faulted breccia (a rock whose components have angular edges)

skill level: 3

equipment needed: flashlights and/or head lamps are a must; hard hats are a good idea whenever you go underground, but they're not absolutely necessary here so long as you go slowly, watching your footing and also the ceiling

temperature: influenced by ambient temperature

tour length: plan on at least 2–4 hours, depending on the caves you pick

description: There are two primary caves in the park. Balconies Cave is nearer to the west entrance, while Bear Gulch Cave is closer to the east. The primary difference is Bear Gulch is closed mid-May to mid-July to provide peace and quiet for the colony of Townsend's big-eared bats. There is a gate about half-way into the Bear Gulch Cave to allow folks access to much of the cave during the rest of the year and at certain times the entire cave is open for exploration. But you have to check the schedule on the website if you want to be sure.

By contrast, few bats live in Balconies Cave and it is almost always open. It does, however, sometimes close in the rainy season due to flooding. These are among the largest and longest talus caves in the country. They're a must-see for serious cavers who are looking for variety to add to their cave log. Rarely do such caves get more than a few dozen feet. But these are so long that they close out the light completely and place you in a real cave scenario.

directions: There are two entrances to this park and there is no road connecting the two. So take your pick on which side you want to park at. East Entrance—From King City follow 1st Street NE as it becomes Bitterwater Road (County G13). Follow Bitterwater Road about 14 miles until it intersects Highway 25. Turn left on Highway 25 (north) and follow for approximately 15 miles. Turn left onto Highway 146 to enter the monument. West Entrance—From Soledad take Highway 146 east 14 miles into Pinnacles National Monument.

precautions: Be careful of uneven footing, low ceilings and unpredictable drops. Some areas around the caves are dangerous despite their benign appearance.

geology

Both caves are very similar, having formed in essentially the same manner. Both were subjected to the most outrageous abuses in recorded geologic time. Imagine, if you will, a peaceful geologic community living quietly in the suburbs of a large volcanic complex. Things are going along just fine until one day about 23 million years ago Mr. Volcano himself announces he's decided to erupt. Well, everyone is thinking, la-de-da, the volcano is gonna erupt, so what! Turns out this isn't your run-of-the-mill cry-baby eruption. Instead, it's one of those mega-volcanic tizzy fits that result in a tumultuous upheaval of the whole area. Not only does lava come pouring out in floods, but the entire region shakes and becomes unglued. Giant landslides wash whole communities away in a torrent of rock, ash, lava, mud and mobile home parts. When everything subsides, you're left with a total mess. The end result is the Pinnacles Volcanic Formation (PVF) consisting of massive pile-ups of volcanic debris. But the story of woe doesn't stop there: Over the next few decamillion years, aggressive faulting thugs continuously barged in and out, uprooting solid-rock neighborhoods and throwing things all over the place. The PVF has been continually subjected to such severe geologic injustices that the World Geohealth Organization has called on the international community to put an end to the violence. For now, at least, there is relative peace.

The outside is even better than the inside.

Yep, there's sure a lot of rocks piled up here! But if it wasn't for that we'd not have any caves here.

ABOVE: *Even if you aren't into caves, this place has copious amounts of great hiking trails.*

RIGHT: *For those of you into bouldering, Pinnacles has plenty of problems to offer you.*

ABOVE: *Not far from the west side picnic area is the Balconies Cave which sometimes has water running through it.*

RIGHT: *There are literally hundreds of routes and several guidebooks published on the climbing here.*

BELOW: *Another beautiful sight.*

Pinnacles is a famous climbing area. When you see the spectacular cliffs and spires, you'll understand why.

IF YOU GO . . .

contact info: Pinnacles Visitor Center and Pinnacles Campground,
   phone: 831-389-4485; www.nps.gov/pinn/index.htm
fee: per vehicle fee
hours: east side is open 24/7; west side is open daylight hours only
lodging: camping available only on east side; lodging in King City or Soledad
aboveground: great hiking trails in one of the most scenic parks in the region;
   excellent rock climbing with hundreds of routes of varying difficulties

26

Pluto's Cave

type of site: a single long, large lava tube

skill level: 3

equipment needed: although you could get by with just a flashlight, basic caving equipment is strongly advisable—hard hat with head lamp, flashlights and gloves; good boots and rugged clothing also recommended

temperature: most of this site is influenced by ambient temperatures; but some of the deeper parts are in the 50s

tour length: at least 2–4 hours, but it could be more, considering the great views of Mt. Shasta

description: Ever walked inside a lava flow? You should if you haven't, but make it "a tall cold one." Lucky for you, there are many of them around here, but Pluto's Cave is one of the best and it's big enough that you can walk upright inside most of its half-mile passage. This long, interesting tunnel was formed roughly 190,000 years ago by molten rock that erupted from a volcanic vent. The top, sides, and bottom of the flow cooled and solidified first, after which the inside emptied out like a straw, leaving behind the present cave. It seems the cave was named after the Roman God of the underworld by the first white man to see it—a fellow named Nelson Cash, who discovered it 1863 while looking for stray cattle. However, there's plenty of evidence that Native Americans were using this cave for thousands of years before that, although you'd be hard put to find any evidence of that now with all the graffiti and trash left behind by the local party animals.

directions: From Weed, drive north on Highway 97 approximately 12.5 miles to the Grenada turnoff (county road A12). Turn left and head northwest for 3.5 miles to a telephone pole on your left that is marked "Pluto Caves." Turn here and follow this road about 0.3 miles to the parking area which also has a picnic table.

precautions: Rough footing and precarious, balanced rock piles in places. The lava can be sharp and unforgiving if you run against it.

geology

John Muir, who himself visited this place in the late 1800s, would not be a happy camper if he saw what's been going on here as of late. He'd cringe and probably get mighty angry once he saw all the graffiti and trash at this place. Generations of bozos have scratched and spray painted all kinds of childish symbols along part of the walls. If that wasn't enough, they've also thrown trash all over. But you can help set things straight! Please consider spreading some good karma by bringing a plastic trash bag or two (Julie and I carry a few plastic grocery bags with us for just such a purpose) and carry out some garbage. Many folks have already got into this praise-worthy act and in the last few years there has been progress. Let's stick to it! Pluto's Cave will get cleaned up and Mother Earth will smile again.

Neon graffiti on the walls inside the main lava tube. Please help us to uphold the dignity of nature—collect litter and refrain from such childish desecration.

Pluto's cave is one of the biggest lava tubes you can access in the state of California.

IF YOU GO . . .

contact info: Goosenest Ranger District, phone: 530-398-439;
www.northbankfred.com/pluto.html

fee: no fee, so how about visiting the Siskiyou County Museum in Yreka
and making a donation there?

hours: daylight hours

lodging: basic camping in Shasta-Trinity National Forest; lodging in Weed

aboveground: great hiking trails here and just south; superb views of Mt.
Shasta right from the entrance area

27

Sixteen to One Mine

type of site: active underground gold mine with aboveground museum

skill level: 3

equipment needed: it is wet and cool in the mine, so long pants and a light jacket are recommended; also bring waterproof shoes if you have them, or borrow a pair from the museum; bring a flashlight and day-pack with water as well

temperature: about 50 degrees year-round

tour length: underground tours are customized for each group and may focus on a variety of mining and geology topics; the *Excursion* Tour lasts 3–4 hours; *Miner for a Day* is available weekdays only; it's a full day with the miners customized to the interests and abilities of participant

description: In this adventure you'll experience California's gold mining history through a mine that has been in operation for over a century. Established in 1896, the Sixteen to One Mine is a unique "pocket" mine where gold is found in highly concentrated deposits within the quartz vein. The 3–4 hour tour begins at the museum where you will be introduced to the history of the Alleghany Mining District and the operation at the Sixteen to One Mine. From there, groups carpool to the Sixteen to One portal on Kanaka Creek (down a dirt road) where you "brass in" and begin the trip underground. The world of the traditional hard-rock gold miner and the geology of the mine are witnessed first-hand. Tours travel into the mine as far as the 800 Station (about 1,200 feet) and back another 1,000 feet to the Tightner Shaft and then to the active workings.

directions: The mine is located in the town of Alleghany, about 18 miles east of Route 49 in Camptonville. Tours usually start at the mine museum on Main Street. In some cases they start right at the mine itself. Exact directions will be provided when you register for the tour.

precautions: Bring waterproof shoes if you have them. Bring a flashlight and day-pack with water as well. All tours require the ability to navigate steep rough terrain on foot. This is a working mine— there are few modifications made in the facilities to provide for "tourists."

geology

This mine has 30 miles of tunnels and penetrates over 3000' into the side of the mountain. Over the years, the 16:1 Mine has produced 1 million ounces of gold. But it's most famous for its quartz and gold mineral specimens sought by collectors and jewelers. The native gold is trapped in solid quartz and is mined in the "rough" that way. When a well-concentrated "pocket" is discovered, instead of crushing the ore, they prepare the specimen using acids that break down the quartz but do not affect the gold. This results in stunning mineral specimens of pure gold, many of which are mounted naturally on their white quartz matrix. One such piece, "The Whopper," is the largest such specimen in the company collection. It weighs approximately 13 pounds and contains an estimated 140 troy ounces of pure gold.

This is a true working mine where you'll be seeing the real McCoy of hard-rock gold mining.

Some of the traditional mine buildings still stand on the site in the hills near the picturesque historic town of Alleghany.

IF YOU GO . . .

contact info: tours offered by Sierra Gold, phone: 530-289-1621;
   16:1 Mine general information, phone: 530-287-3330;
   www.undergroundgold.com and www.origsix.com
fee: per-person fee, group rates available
hours: May–October by reservation only; call to book tours two weeks ahead
lodging: camping in Tahoe National Forest; lodging in Downieville
aboveground: excellent museum associated with the mine; Alleghany
   is an historic town with some interesting buildings

28

Subway Cave

type of site: single large underground lava tube with interpretive stations

skill level: 2

equipment needed: it's fairly cool here, so take a jacket; you'll also need flashlights and/or head lamps

temperature: constant 46 degrees

tour length: self-guided—about 1 hour

description: This is one of the best lava tubes in North America and it's an easy, short hike. So if you are in the area, get some real underground kicks at this incredible place. From the parking area it's a quick hike up to the entrance where steps take you down under. The course then follows one-way inside the broad tube for about ⅓ of a mile. As you explore the area with your flashlight you suddenly notice a bright reflection or two in the darkness. Upon investigation you'll find they are nifty little educational stations the U.S. Forest Service has installed at several points along the tunnel. Since there are no significant branchings in this tube section, you cannot get lost. At the other end there's another set of steps leading out into the sunshine.

Lava tubes are not really rare. In fact, they are pretty common in areas of past or present volcanic activity. But when you've seen lots of them like we have, you are always on the lookout for something unique. And this one has it! The walls of this tube are the smoothest we've ever seen in such a large and long stretch—they really do look like a subway tunnel.

directions: To reach the cave, head north on California 89 from its intersection with 44 at Old Station (which is about 60 miles east of Redding). The parking area is on the east (right) side after about 0.3 miles, across the road from the Cave Campground.

precautions: The floor is a bit rough so we advise sturdy shoes or boots. Most of the tube has pretty high ceilings, but there are places where it has low points so go slowly and watch your head.

geology

Hats off to Hat Creek! A mere 20,000 years ago they put on a marvelous show here—one of those legendary rock concerts you hear old timers brag about. The scene was hot! Just as soon as the "Hat Creek Flow" started up the magma machine, the crowd went wild. The Fissures, a local band of some repute, started spewing voluminous amounts of raucous lava from a series of north-south cracks in the earth not far from here. Thus introduced, the notorious Lava River Band got a little hammered while hanging out in saloons near the town of Old Station, but eventually crawled northward 16 miles, covering the floor of Hat Creek Valley with black magma as it went. While the top crust cooled and hardened, rivers of red-hot lava continued to flow below. But then the Fissures petered out, the Lava River Band left the stage, and Hat Creek Flow passed out en masse, abruptly ending the gnarly party. The liquid lava below drained away like so many rock-n-roll groupies after the band blows town. The resulting vacancy created tube-shaped caves in the lava flow. Subway Cave is the largest accessible tube in this flow. Its entrance was formed by a partial collapse of the cave's roof many years ago. Its walls and roof are smooth and rounded. And, in case you're wondering, it does look like a subway, but without the trains.

Easy access is provided by stairways into and out of the cave.

It really does look like a subway. But the good news is you don't have to buy a ticket or wait in line during rush hour.

IF YOU GO . . .

contact info: Lassen National Forest Hat Creek Ranger District, phone: (530) 336-5521; http://www.fs.fed.us/r5/lassen/recreation/hatcreek/subway.php

fee: no fee

hours: daylight hours May through October; closed in winter

lodging: camping right across the road at Cave Campground; closest lodging is in Shingletown and Redding

aboveground: be sure to visit the Spatter Cones Trail, a brand new educational loop created in the lava fields just south of here; to reach it, head south on California 89 from its intersection with 44 at Old Station (just west of Subway Cave); parking is on the east (left) side, about 1.5 miles

29

Sunny Jim Sea Cave

type of site: historic, famous sea cave accessed via an underground tunnel

skill level: 2

equipment needed: no special equipment necessary

temperature: influenced by ambient temperatures

tour length: self-guided—generally about 1 hour or less inside, but you'll want to enjoy the outside as well, so figure at least 2 hours minimum

description: Once you enter the Cave Store you're stepping into a piece of history. The building, one of the older unmodified structures in town, is nearly a century old. It was erected in 1920 and has remained pretty much the way you see it since construction. Even the sign is historic. The tunnel that leads to the sea cave is even older—having been dug by hand in 1903. As soon as you approach the entrance of the tunnel, you hear the rumble of the sea far below. It is an altogether thrilling sound to hear that inside a building that is situated far up on dry land.

The trip down to the cave used to be a slip-sliding adventure on the mud floor of the tunnel. Patrons used rings driven into the tunnel walls to help hoist themselves back out. But then somebody invented the stairway. The trip now involves 145 short steps to reach the bottom and is facilitated by a hand rail. The tunnel is lighted, so you really don't need anything else except a camera to enjoy this place.

directions: Sunny Jim Sea Cave is accessed via a tunnel inside the historic Cave Store located near Coast Blvd. at 1325 Cave Street, right on the cliffs at La Jolla Cove.

precautions: The stairs are usually wet and can be slippery. Keep a hold of the railing. As inviting as it may seem, DO NOT attempt to go outside the deck. It's very dangerous and the sea can give you a thrashing without notice.

Sunny Jim Sea Cave

Gustav Schultz may seem to some folks an enterprising, West Coast version of P.T. Barnum but there's a big difference; he never thought of people as suckers and he never attempted to cheat anyone. Yet he was an entrepreneur, even before the term was coined, and he read with interest newspaper stories of exotic underground expeditions taking place way off in the Sierras. Tourists of the day (late 1800s) were all ga-ga about seeing the underworld. They traveled hundreds of miles and, most importantly, paid to see them. Gustav was intrigued. But he wasn't about to go traipsing way inland to some god-forsaken mountains in search of a hole in the ground. He liked the ocean and was staying put here along the shore. The problem was, there weren't any caves around southern California. Or were there?

Once the proverbial light went on in Gustav's head, there was no dimming it. He bought some land and hired cheap Chinese labor to excavate a tunnel at just the right angle to allow access to the sea caves below. He installed rings in the walls to facilitate getting back up. (After all, it wouldn't be good for business if you had only a one-way flow of patrons into the ocean.) It wasn't long before Gustav Schultz had cornered the market on underground tours all along the southern California coast.

The long series of steps down into the ground culminate in a unique experience where you end up inside the belly of a bona fide sea cave without having to swim.

Don't worry, when the seas get too rough they close the tours until things have settled down.

IF YOU GO . . .

contact info: Sunny Jim Cave Store, phone: 858-459-0746
fee: per-person fee; group rates available
hours: open every day except Christmas and New Year's Day; hours vary with season
lodging: improved camping and lodging in immediate area, but lodging in La Jolla is gonna set you back apiece
aboveground: the Cave Store has gifts, historical photos and memorabilia; a walk along the cliffs is especially scenic in the evening; there's a beautiful view from atop the cliffs looking down to the natural cave opening below; also some great coffee and fine dining in the immediate area

30

Sutter Gold Mine

type of site: modern underground gold mine

skill level: 1.5

equipment needed: you'll be provided a hard hat before heading down

temperature: a pleasant 65 degrees year round

tour length: guided tour takes about one hour

description: Wanna buy a gold mine? You just might be able to if you can scrape together the pocket change—say $30 million or so. Sutter Gold Mining Company is a relatively new mine that follows a vein into the hill just outside of the quaint little town of Sutter Creek. Following years of planning and construction, the mine started operations as a bona fide producer of gold ore in 1989. Six months after the first trucks brought medium grade ore to the surface, the price of gold dropped and the mine suspended operations. Rumor has it the place is up for sale, but thankfully tours are still allowed.

After a brief introduction on the surface, you board a "Boss Buggy" mine car that takes you down into the main tunnel. Along the way a friendly and very knowledgeable guide introduces some of modern mining's arsenal of toys—various trucks and ore haulers, drills, excavators, and other equipment. You convene in a safety room and learn about the mining process. Then you tour along the active working face itself, following the vein, and are introduced to the geology of gold in general and of this locale in particular. You even get a chance to see native gold flecks in the bedrock before reloading into the car and heading back to the surface. Now that you know something of the mining business, check with your accountant and see if you can buy this place.

directions: Located just north of Sutter Creek, off old California 49. Note: The new Highway 49 bypass takes you around Historic Highway 49 from Sutter Creek to Amador City. To get to Sutter Gold Mine, you must be on Historic Highway 49. From the south, make a right turn on "Old Highway 49." From the north, 2 miles south of Drytown, take the left turn lane with the sign that says "Amador City & Sutter Creek."

precautions: Please don't jump out of the mine car when it's moving. It can inflict serious damage to your body and watch your head in low areas!

history

When opportunity knocks—some people are destined to be trampled beneath it. Take for instance the tragic story of John Augustus Sutter. In the 1840s, Sutter moved to California (at the time part of Mexico), secured a land grant from the Mexican government, and set about becoming a business tycoon. In 1848, a foreman at his sawmill on American Creek found a handful of gold nuggets in the nearby river. He brought the precious pebbles to his boss. Sutter became immediately paranoid of the potential disruption to his fledgling business; he had no experience in gold prospecting. So he hatched a plan to suppress the discovery, but in a few weeks word had spread; soon the entire nation was ignited in the California Gold Rush.

Paradoxically, the one man best positioned to take advantage of the rich gold deposits of the Sierras never reaped the benefits. Sutter lost the chance to capitalize on the find near his mill. In a belated attempt to cash in on the discovery, Sutter organized a prospecting team but was soon forced to abandon the idea. Later, his mill was destroyed by hordes of prospectors, his crops were trampled, and his storehouses were raided. Sutter watched his businesses evaporate. Ruined and dispirited, he abandoned California. To add insult to injury, in 1858 the US decided Sutter's land grant was invalid, effectively erasing any claim he had to the property.

This is a modern mine which is poised to start working again.

This is one of the most authentic modern hard-rock mine tours in California. You load onto "boss buggies" to tour the underground.

ABOVE: *There's not much walking on this tour, but you do get to visit some of the gold-bearing veins as well as the "Safe Room"*

RIGHT: *Some of the drilling equipment used to bore holes for setting charges.*

Sutter Gold Mine

ABOVE: *The entrance leads into the side of the hill.*

RIGHT: *Inside, you'll see where the working vein is exposed. You'll even see real flecks of native gold in the ceilings and walls.*

BELOW: *When you see the sign, you know you're there!*

Aboveground there are collections of old mining equipment and machinery as well as a chance at gold panning.

IF YOU GO . . .

contact info: Sutter Gold Mine, phone: (866) 762-2837;
www.caverntours.com/sgmtmap.html

fee: per-person fee; group rates available

hours: open every day except Christmas and New Year's Day; hours vary with season

lodging: camping at Indian Grinding Rock SHP; lodging in Sutter Creek

aboveground: visitor center, movie theater, picnic area; located near Sutter Creek, a quaint historic town with shops, galleries and great food

References / Websites / Resources

References

Cave Geology, Palmer, Arthur N., 2007, National Speleological Society, Huntsville, AL.

Great Caves of the World, Waltham, Tony, 2008, Firefly Books, Tonawanda, NY.

Hidden Beneath the Mountains: The Caves of Sequoia and Kings Canyon National Parks, Despain, Joel, 2003, Cave Books, Trenton, NJ.

Roadside Geology of Northern and Central California, 2001, Alt, David, Mountain Press Publishing Company, Missoula, MT.

Caves of Fire: Inside America's Lava Tubes, Bunnell, D. 2008, National Speleological Society, Huntsville, AL.

Websites

National Speleological Society:
www.caves.org/

National Speleological Society, San Francisco Bay chapter:
www.caves.org/grotto/sfbc/

California Geological Survey:
www.conservation.ca.gov/CGS/Pages/Index.aspx

Good Earth Graphics:
www.goodearthgraphics.com/virtcave

Websites Referenced in Text

Several sites in this book benefited from text from specific websites, which was used with the permission of their respective owners:

Sierra Nevada Recreation Corporation
www.caverntours.com/

Sequoia Natural History Association
www.sequoiahistory.org

California State Mining and Mineral Museum
www.parks.ca.gov/?page_id=588

Boyden Cavern
www.caverntours.com/BoydenRt.htm

Original Sixteen to One Mine, Inc.
www.origsix.com

Glossary

archaeology Why are you asking me this? You should know it already! It's basically the study of ancient cultures, their remains, artifacts, structures, and influences.

Archaic In North America, the native cultures that predate the ancestral pueblo peoples (Hisatsinom) but occur after Clovis time. The Archaic period is roughly defined as running from about 6,000 BC to about 900 BC.

basalt It's old lava—simple as that.

batholith The word separates nicely into bath-o-lith, which is useful in remembering its meaning. In Greek, the term *bath* refers to a body which is warmed and, *lith* refers to rock. A batholith is a giant bubble of magma that never extrudes out the crust but eventually cools and hardens below the surface.

calcite The most common crystalline form of calcium carbonate. Calcite is a very abundant rock-forming mineral in sedimentary rocks and also the primary mineral component of limestone and marble.

desert patina/desert varnish The effect is as if some cosmic woodworker spilled a very large bucket of dark stain over the desert floor, coating all the exposed rock on the surface. That stain is comprised mostly of iron oxides that color the outer surface dark brown to black, while the inside is the natural rock color, usually much lighter.

dike or dyke Instead of a homophobic slur, this is a geologic descriptor for igneous material which intrudes into other rocks in a more-or-less vertical orientation. If the surrounding rock is softer and erodes away, the dyke sticks up, often forming sharp ridges.

geoglyph A singularly cool archeological site made by either aligning/piling rocks into designs and shapes, or, alternatively, by deliberate removal of stones from an area creating recognizable patterns in the ground during the process.

geology A very cool and hip career if you can make a living at it, which most geology graduates have a hard time doing, myself included. The term refers to the study of the Earth and the processes that continue to shape it.

hard rock No, it's not a cafe. OK, so it IS a cafe, but that has nothing to do with what we're talking about here. In this case it's a geology and mining term referring mostly to metamorphic and igneous rock.

helictite One of the stranger cave formations. Helictites obviously have no respect for gravity and grow at improbable angles up, down, and sideways. The exact mechanics of their growth are not understood and many theories have been posited to explain how they form. Some think helictites form because of capillary action, whereas others hold that solution micropressures, changeable cave air currents, or distorted crystal growth are the cause for their strange appearance.

hog-back Another crazy geology term coined by a geologist who thought he saw some semblance of animal physiology in a pile of rocks that stood on end.

igneous Rock which forms more-or-less directly from a molten state.

karst Here we go again with those wacky geologic terms. Karst refers to landforms characterized by surface sinkholes, ravines, depressions and, most of all, subterranean cavities (caves). Karst usually forms in areas of high calcium and gypsum rock such as limestone and marble which is easily eroded by water solutions traveling through it. The term comes from a limestone plateau by the same name near Trieste, Italy where this phenomenon is especially apparent.

lava You should know this already, but here's a little more info for ya: Yes, we all know this is volcanic in origin. But lava need not have come from a stereotypical volcano. It often arrives by out-pouring from large cracks in Earth's crust.

lava tube A natural "tube" that forms when a lava "river" exits from a its subsurface channel in a lava flow, leaving a roofed-over tunnel in its place. In highly volcanic areas lava tubes are often very abundant.

lithology Refers to rock, and I don't mean rock-and-roll bands. Rather it's all about stony rock—the different types, their composition, and the processes that produce them. Also can mean the subdivision of geology which studies rock.

magma Molten rock or lava before it has cooled. Don't tangle with this stuff.

metamorphic A classification of rock which forms by subjecting parent rock to intense heat and pressure thereby altering its chemistry without completely melting it. Sort of like what happens to parents as they raise kids.

metate Stone grinding surface used by native cultures to pulverize corn and other plant material.

PaleoIndian Term given to all ancestral Indians that predate well-documented dominant native cultures. In North America this generally refers to any pre-Clovis peoples older than about 8,000 years.

paleontology The study of fossils, which, in turn, has nothing to do with the watch-making company of the same name.

pegmatite Another nebulous geologic term which loosely defines a diverse group of coarse-crystal granites that are high in quartz and feldspar and often occur in veins or dikes. If you suspect you've got some on your property, you'll be happy to know they're also a good place to look for gold.

petroglyph In Greek, *Petro* means rock, *glyph* means form. This term also references the way in which the image is made—etched or inscribed into the rock face by pecking away the outer surface.

pictograph Meaningful painting on rocks by ancient cultures. (As opposed to meaningless painting on subway cars, which we scientists call "graffiti.")

pueblo Pueblo is a term used to denote a communal building structure that generally houses multiple families and is the center of activity for a given community.

riparian Has nothing to do with repairing anything. Refers to natural environments that abide along permanent waterways. Home to wildlife galore.

rhyolite It can be spooky—Rhyolite is a ghost town in Nevada. Oh, by the way, it's also a volcanic rock high in silica, something of an extrusive equivalent to granite.

sedimentary My sentiments about sediments: They're pretty cool rocks which form as accumulations of particles from the break-down of other rocks.

selective weathering/selective erosion The key here is "selective," like "selective service" when Uncle Sam calls you up for military duty. Certain rocks are softer than others and erode away much faster, leaving the harder, more durable, rock to stand out.

shield volcano Refers to a volcano that doesn't look anything at all like a volcano. The term comes from a translation of the name for a certain volcano in Iceland called *Skjaldbreiður* which means "broad shield." Shield volcanoes have very gradual, gently-sloping sides and vents and cinder cones are often found on their sides.

sink If you're thinking of the catchment basins in your house then you're not too far off. Now imagine a depression in the ground which effectively performs similarly to your kitchen sink and you've got it. If that depression collapses into a steep-walled hole, now you've got a sinkhole.

soft rock We are not referring to elevator music or "smooth jazz" here. The sedimentary rock to which this term applies is usually not as hard as its counterparts in the metamorphic or igneous realm. So if it comes to throws, bet on the hard rock—it'll kick soft rock's butt every time.

solution cave A type of cave that forms by dissolution of matrix (base) rock, usually from mildly acidic water (solutions). Most solution caves are in limestone and marble, rock which is susceptible to attack by acids. Also refers to holes in the ground, which solve the problem of certain modern-day troglodytes (cavers) seeking adventure below the surface.

speleothems Remember how I said in America the sport is called "caving," not "spelunking?" Well, that's that. EXCEPT that some of the terminology refers back to the European roots of going underground. The term refers to cave formations, usually those occurring in limestone or marble caverns.

spheroidal weathering Sometimes the weather gets crappy and you're stuck just riding it out. Same thing happens in this case except that "you" happen to be rock, often granite, which gets weathered in such a way as to round off its edges. As things progress the weathering rounds off the rounded edges. And it keeps going round and round and . . . well, you get the idea.

strata/stratigraphy Another fancy geology term used to confound unsuspecting party-goers. Basically refers to layers of rock and the arrangement of those layers.

stratovolcano Your typical run-of-the-mill, tall, cone-shaped photogenic volcano. Any volcano worth his salt would join the ranks of Team Strato.

troglodyte Don't take it personally, but if you are fairly primitive and like to live in seclusion—especially in a cave—then you're a troglodyte. But it's not all bad. You probably don't have to pay for air-conditioning, do you?

volcanic bomb It's not something likely to turn up in Transportation Safety Administration (TSA) checks of luggage at the airports, but you never know. When a volcano explodes and hurls liquid magma skyward, the globs cool and harden as they fly through the air, developing tell-tale shapes before hitting the ground or clueless bystanders.

window If you had a solid wall on your house that you wanted to let the sun shine through, what would you do? Smash a hole in the sucker, of course. That bit of handiwork is called a window. Now let me ask you, why should Mother Nature shy away from doing the same thing when she wants to have sunlight stream through a hard-rock wall?

Index

V

W

About the Authors

Jon Kramer is an adventurer first, and also a geologist, writer, climber and surfer (but not necessarily in that order, depending on the surf). He received his Bachelor of Science degree in geology at the University of Maryland and has pursued life as an adventuring paleontologist ever since. His interests are quite varied and include all things natural. In addition to popular travel and adventure writing, Jon  has published scientific papers on critters as ancient as 2 billion-year-old bacteria and as young as 12,000-year-old mammoths. Jon travels extensively with his wife Julie, sometimes settling down for a rest in Minnesota, Florida, California and interesting points in between.

Julie Martinez is an explorer, naturalist, freelance artist and formal art instructor. Her appreciation for insects, plants, rocks and fossils started in childhood with a collection that has grown throughout her life. Julie graduated from the University of Wisconsin, Stevens Point, with a degree in Fine Arts and Biology. She initially worked as an illustrator for the medical field but in the late 1980s began a freelance career,  which she has enjoyed ever since. Julie's work is featured in many textbooks, journals and museum exhibits throughout North America. She is also a staff teacher at Minnesota School of Botanical Art. When not teaching, she travels with Jon, exploring the wilds of the world.